CLEAR & SIMPLE

SPANISH

MARY WILLIX FARMER

A MONARCH BOOK
Published by Prentice Hall Press
New York, NY 10023

A Monarch Book
Published by Prentice Hall Press
A Division of Simon & Schuster, Inc.
Gulf+Western Building
One Gulf+Western Plaza
New York, New York 10023

PRENTICE HALL PRESS is a trademark of Simon & Schuster, Inc.

Designed by Mike Kelly, San Diego, California
Produced by The Word Shop, Inc., San Diego, California
Manufactured in the United States of America

2   3   4   5   6   7   8   9   10

Library of Congress Catalog Card Number: 85-062456
ISBN: 0-671-54660-0

CONTENTS

ACKNOWLEDGMENT

The author is grateful to Ferne McCuen, Spanish teacher at La Jolla Country Day School, La Jolla, California, for her help with grammar exercises and editing.

THE SOUND SYSTEM

It's important for you to know the sounds of Spanish and to pronouce them correctly right from the beginning. It's easier to learn correct pronunciation now than to change bad habits later.

THE VOWELS

Spanish Vowel System

i (piso)	u (puso)	**high**
e (peso)	o (poso)	**mid**
	a (paso)	**low**

front   mid   back

The diagram above is known as the Vowel Triangle. It indicates where in the mouth the tongue should be as each vowel is pronounced. Pronouncing vowels is very simple in Spanish. Because it's so simple, it may be difficult for you if you are a native speaker of American English. A so-called normalized system of English vowels has 17 vowel nuclei and numerous diphthongs (a single syllable with two vowel sounds). Vowel sounds vary widely among dialects. You'll need to concentrate to keep the Spanish vowels simple and clear. Look at these Spanish-English sound-alikes:

a   Spanish /a/ (papa) sounds like English "a" as in "father."

o   Spanish /o/ (poco) sounds like English "o" as in "boat," but it is never diphthongized as English /o/ is. Notice how English "no" ends with a /u/ sound.

e   Spanish /e/ (de) sounds like English "a" as in "Kate."

i   Spanish /i/ (si) sounds like English "ee" as in "sweet."

u   Spanish /u/ (puso) sounds like the "u" in English "sue."

The five Spanish vowels may occur by themselves or in combination with /y/ or /w/ (a written "u"), allowing a total of 13 possible combinations. However, only 10 of these combinations are used frequently.

All five Spanish vowels occur in stressed and unstressed syllables without significant change in phonetic quality. But in English only three vowel sounds occur regularly under weak stress (front, central, and back) though each has a fairly wide range. Notice the change in the vowel quality of the letter "o" when "suppose" is changed to "supposition." The same sort of change takes place with the letter "a" when "able" is changed to "ability."

Since the sounds of Spanish vowels are the same for stressed and unstressed syllables, practice saying the following two words, making the vowels in the second syllable clearly different:

hable   habla

THE CONSONANTS

Spain Versus Spanish America

Though there are numerous dialects of Spanish, the two most commonly recognized are referred to as CECEO (pronounced "thetheo") and SESEO. The CECEO is used in northern and central Spain (and certain parts of the south), and the SESEO is used in parts of southern Spain and in Spanish America. What distinguishes one from the other is the treatment of the following written symbols: "z", "ci", and "ce". Speakers of the CECEO dialect use a θ (*theta*), a sound that occurs in English as a written "th" as in the words "thin" and "ether." It is voiceless, contrasting with the sound we use in the words "then" and "either," which is voiced. Several other regional differences will be mentioned under individual consonant sounds.

Formation of Consonants

l

English has two "l" sounds. Spanish has only one. If you say the word "little" you'll feel both English "l" sounds. The first "l" is made in the front of the mouth, and the second is made in the back. In Spanish, only a front "l" is used. Practice the following Spanish words using a front "l":

sal   tal   del   hotel

ll, y

The "ll" and the "y" tend to be pronounced the same, both as [y], in most of the Spanish-speaking world. (The "y" pronunciation is called *yeísmo*.) However, there are variations. They may be pronounced as the initial sound in the English word "judge" or the central sound in the English word "measure." These pronunciations are common in Argentina. Individual speakers may vary in their treatment of these symbols. Some Spaniards give "ll" an [ly] sound, as in English "million."

h

The letter "h" is never pronounced. It is the only silent letter in Spanish.

ñ

This letter is called "eñe," and it is essentially a combination of [n] and [y], similar to the "ny" in "canyon," but produced as one sound.

x

An "x" before a consonant is pronounced [s]. Between vowels it is pronounced [ks]. Several Spanish words conserve an old Spanish spelling when an "x" was pronounced as a [j], notably in the words "Don Quixote" and "México." In areas where Spanish has come into contact with Indian languages, an "x" may have alternate pronunciations, particularly in place names — for example, Xochimilco ("x" is an [s]) and Uxmal ("x" is the same as English "sh").

p, t, k

These sounds are not aspirated in Spanish. This means they do not have the breathiness that English "p," "t," and "k" have. In English they may be highly aspirated in some positions. Put your hand in front of your mouth and feel the aspiration (breathiness) when you say

pop   cat   cook

Now say some Spanish words that have these three consonants and try to control the aspiration. You'll need to tighten the muscles around your mouth. Say

papa   por   catedral   paquete

r, rr   Spanish has both a trill (/rr/) and a flap (/r/), and the pronunciation of these two phonemes is sometimes a problem for English speakers. The trill is a series of strikes made by the tongue on the ridge behind the upper teeth (the alveolar ridge). Put your tongue in the place where you make a "d." You must be relaxed to do it. (If you try too hard, you may become tense and have no luck at all.) The trill is used in the following situations:

Initial **r**	radio, rancho, Ramon
Medial double **r**	carro, perro, corro
r before a consonant	parte, corto, Marta
Final **r** (slight)	motor, hablar, vivir

The flap occurs when there is a single "r" between vowels. This sound occurs in American English as a "tt" or "dd" in medial position. Say the words "butter," "wedding," and "potter" in English in a very relaxed manner and notice how your tongue is flapping on the roof of your mouth. The sound it is making is neither a [t] nor a [d]. It is the same as a Spanish flap.

Now you're ready to try some Spanish words with the same sound: **para, pero, coro, caro**. Now try alternating from a trill to a flap:

caro	carro
coro	corro
pero	perro

b, d, g   These three letters each have two possible sounds. They are grouped together for explanation because the pronunciation and circumstances for the alternate sound have something in common. Each one has a stop variant, that is, a pronunciation that stops the air flow, and a pronunciation that continues the air flow. The first set of sounds is nearly the same as those we have in English. The "b" is like the English /b/ in "boy." The "d" is made on the back of the teeth, rather than higher up on the alveolar ridge as we do in English. The "g" is like the /g/ in "go." These variants are used after a pause, after "n," and after "l."

The alternate sounds do not stop the flow of air. They will be represented here with bars through the letters:

[b̶]   [d̶]   [g̶]

The only one of these sounds that occurs in English is the [đ], which is the same as the English "th" in "then" and "either." The other two do not exist in English. However, if a [g̶] is extreme, it sounds like an English "w." (For most Spanish speakers the letter "v" is pronounced the same as a "b.")

[d]	**[đ]**
dar	lado
donde	usted
falda	ciudad

[b]	**[b̶]**
boca	cabo
beca	tuvo

[g]	**[g̶]**
guante	agua
gato	lago

z   In Spanish, a "z" is pronounced [s].

zebra   [sebra]

Note that the letter "s" is also pronounced [s]. In English, a medial "s" is often pronounced [z]. Note the following contrasts between English medial "s" and Spanish medial "s."

[z]	**[s]**
rose	rosa
president	presidente

j, g   The letter "j" is pronounced [h] or as a more guttural [x]. The sound may vary from speaker to speaker as well as within the speech of an individual. The "g" has the same pronunciation as the "j" before the letters "e" and "i." It is a stop (or "hard" sound, as it is sometimes called) before "u," "a," and "o."

[h] or **[x]**	**[g]**
Jorge	gato
general	gota
gitano	guerra

Nasals   In Spanish, nasals ("m," "n," "ñ") are made in the same place as the consonant following them, as they are in certain English cases. This means that an "n" is not always made by placing the tongue behind the teeth. It may be made in other parts of the mouth. If you say the English word "finger," you will feel that the "n" is made in the back of the mouth, in the same place as the "g." This happens in Spanish, too, not only within words but across word boundaries as well.

chango	[čaŋgo]
un poco	[umpoko]

STRESS   Spanish words that end in a vowel, "n," or "s" have the stress on the next-to-the-last syllable. Accent marks are used to change the natural stress pattern.

Natural stress	*el papa (the Pope)*
Altered stress	*el papá (the dad)*

Accent marks are also used to distinguish homophones from each other. Homophones are distinguished by written accent:

él	he
el	the
sí	yes
si	if

Chapter 2
ARTICLES AND NOUNS

DEFINITE ARTICLES

There are four ways to say "the" in Spanish. Think of place names such as El Paso, Los Angeles, La Mesa, and Las Vegas. You are already familiar with the Spanish articles that occur in these names. Now you just need to know when to use each one. The definite article must agree with the noun it modifies.

Definite Articles

	Singular	Plural
Feminine	la	las
Masculine	el	los

Rules and Examples. Here are some rules for using the definite articles in which their usage differs from English definite articles. You may not feel ready to learn these rules at this point. If not, continue on and return to this section after you finish the section on nouns.

1. **With titles.** The definite article is used before titles when referring to a person, but not when speaking directly to someone.

    La Profesora Sánchez es de Texas.

    El Doctor Smith es veterinario.

    El Licenciado Castellanos es abogado.

    Note. Licenciado is a title that generally refers to attorneys, but in some parts of the Spanish-speaking world, it may mean that a person has a license to practice in one of a variety of fields.

2. **With languages and subjects of study.** The definite article is used with languages and other subjects of study, except after the words **hablar, en,** or **de.** In popular speech there are some exceptions, which we will see later.

Ella estudia el español.	She studies Spanish.
Ella habla español.	She speaks Spanish.
Está escrito en español.	It is written in Spanish.
Él enseña la historia.	He teaches history.

Note. In informal everyday speech the article is commonly omitted with the verbs **aprender** and **estudiar.** For example:

Aprendemos español.	We learn Spanish.
Juan estudia inglés.	John studies English.

1. **With general or abstract nouns.** Spanish uses the definite article before general or abstract nouns, while English does not.

El azúcar es dulce.	Sugar is sweet.
La salud es importante.	Health is important.
Los perros son inteligentes.	Dogs are intelligent.

4. **With the words "iglesia," "clase," and "escuela" when these words follow a preposition.**

Vamos a la iglesia.	We are going to church.
Voy a la clase.	I am going to class.
Aprendemos en la escuela.	We learn at school.

5. **With certain geographic names.**

la Argentina	Argentina	el Paraguay	Paraguay
el Brasil	Brazil	el Perú	Peru
el Ecuador	Ecuador	el Uruguay	Uruguay
el Canadá	Canada		

6. **With days of the week, as a translation for "on."**

No trabajo los miércoles.	I don't work on Wednesdays.
Voy a París el sábado.	I'm going to Paris on Saturday.

INDEFINITE ARTICLES

The indefinite articles "a" and "an" and "some" in Spanish are shown in the following table.

Indefinite Articles

	Singular	Plural
Feminine	una	unas
Masculine	un	unos

Note: The indefinite article is not used after the verb **ser** (to be) when **ser** is followed by an unmodified noun. It is used only when the noun is modified. For example,

Federico García Lorca es poeta.

Juanita Flores es artista.

Gabriel García Márquez es un autor famoso.

Bo Derek es una actriz bonita.

NOUNS

Nouns in Spanish have gender. They are either masculine or feminine. If you have studied Latin or any language derived from Latin (French, Portuguese, or Italian, for example), you are familiar with this concept. If the concept is new to you, simply accept the idea that a table (**mesa**) is feminine and a book (**libro**) is masculine. Nouns that refer to female beings are feminine and nouns that refer to males are masculine, but there is no inherent reason why any inanimate object has one gender rather than the other.

Feminine Nouns

Most nouns ending in -a are feminine. All nouns ending in **-dad, -tad, -tud, -umbre, -ción,** and **-sión** are feminine. In addition, there are other feminine nouns that end in **-e** or a consonant. Nouns that refer to female beings are feminine.

Feminine Nouns Ending in -a

la casa	house	la montaña	mountain
la chica	girl	la cocina	kitchen
la escuela	school	la familia	family
la hermana	sister	la comida	food, dinner
la silla	chair		

Feminine Nouns Ending in -dad, -tad, -tud, -umbre, -ción, -sión

la ciudad	city	la canción	song
la facultad	faculty	la nación	nation
la multitud	multitude	la pasión	passion
la muchedumbre	crowd	la estación	station, season

Nouns That Refer to Female Beings

la mujer	woman	la gata	female cat
la dentista	dentist (f)	la perra	female dog
la doctora	doctor (f)	la agente	agent (f)
la novelista	novelist (f)		

Feminine Nouns Ending in -e

la clase	class	la peste	plague
la madre	mother	la mente	mind
la plebe	populace	la sede	headquarters
la gente	people	la noche	night
la tarde	afternoon, evening		

Note. Some nouns that end in **-e**, such as **estudiante** or **agente**, may be either feminine or masculine. The gender of others must be memorized.

Forming Plurals

Plural Forms

las casas	houses	unas casas	some houses
las chicas	girls	unas chicas	some girls
las ciudades	cities	unas ciudades	some cities
las naciones	nations	unas naciones	some nations

Rule. To pluralize a noun ending in **-a**, simply add **-s**. To pluralize a noun ending in a consonant, add **-es**. Remember to use the plural form of the definite or indefinite article. Words having an accent mark on the last syllable in the singular form drop the accent mark in the plural form.

Exercise A. Make the following feminine nouns plural.

Model: la clase
　　　las clases

1. la madre　　　＿＿＿＿＿＿＿
2. la ciudad　　　＿＿＿＿＿＿＿
3. la escuela　　　＿＿＿＿＿＿＿
4. la facultad　　　＿＿＿＿＿＿＿
5. la montaña　　　＿＿＿＿＿＿＿
6. la familia　　　＿＿＿＿＿＿＿

Masculine Nouns Most nouns that end in **-o** are masculine. Nouns that refer to male beings are masculine. Masculine nouns may also end in a consonant or a vowel other than **-o**. The gender of these nouns must be memorized.

Masculine Nouns Ending in -o

el libro	book	el cuadro	picture
el disco	record	el cuaderno	notebook
el año	year	el chico	boy
el hermano	brother	el tío	uncle
el queso	cheese	el paso	step

Masculine Nouns Ending in -e

el coche	car	el pasaje	passage
el encaje	lace	el despegue	takeoff
el traje	suit	el maquillaje	cosmetics
el guante	glove	el enganche	trap, hook
el nombre	name	el sobre	envelope

Nouns that Refer to Male Beings

el pescador	fisherman	el cura	priest
el dentista	dentist	el hombre	man
el agente	agent	el perro	dog
el estudiante	student	el doctor	doctor

Masculine Nouns Ending in a Consonant

el árbol	tree
el lápiz	pencil
el reloj	clock, watch
el pastel	cake, pastry
el color	color
el cinturón	belt

Exercise B. Make the following masculine nouns plural.

1. el chico _____
2. el coche _____
3. el reloj _____
4. el doctor _____
5. el paso _____

Special Cases

Some Masculine Nouns Ending in -a

el mapa	map	el sistema	system
el drama	play	el tema	theme
el programa	program	el trama	plot

Note. Many of the words in this category came into Spanish from Greek rather than from Latin.

Some Feminine Nouns that End in -o

la mano	hand
la foto	photo
la moto	motorcycle

The last two nouns are actually shortened forms of **la fotografía** and **la motocicleta**.

Feminine Nouns that Begin with a Stressed a- or ha-

el agua	water	las aguas	waters
el águila	eagle	las águilas	eagles
el ancla	anchor	las anclas	anchors
el hacha	ax	las hachas	axes

Rule. The singular form of a feminine word beginning with a stressed **a-** (or **ha-** since the **h** is not pronounced) uses the masculine form of the definite article.

Compound Nouns

Compound nouns are not as common in Spanish as they are in English. One type of Spanish compound noun takes a verb in the second person singular and combines it with a noun in the plural. These compounds are always masculine.

el abrelatas	can opener	el matamoscas	fly swatter
el lavaplatos	dishwasher	el tocadiscos	record player
el rascacielos	skycraper	el lavamanos	washbasin
el parabrisas	windshield	el cuentakilómetros	odomoter

If we look at the composition of the first example, we see **abre** from **abrir** (to open) and **latas** (cans). Each example can be divided between the "a" or "e," which ends the verb portion of the word, and the consonant, which begins the noun portion.

Nouns Whose Meanings Change When the Gender is Changed

la capital	capital (city)	el capital	capital (money)
la cometa	kite	el cometa	comet
la cólera	anger	el cólera	cholera (disease)
la corte	court	el corte	cut
la cura	cure	el cura	priest
la frente	forehead	el frente	front (political or military)
la guía	guidebook	el guía	guide (person)
la orden	order (command, religious)	el orden	order (system)
la policía	police (organization)	el policía	policeman
la vocal	vowel	el vocal	voting member

SUFFIXES

Diminutives

Several endings may be added to Spanish nouns to indicate smallness or endearment. The most common ending is **-ito**, although **-illo** and **ico** are used in some areas. The ending **-ito** is sometimes added to adjectives to soften or diminish their impact (for example, **gordo**, fat; **gordito**, chubby).

casa	house	casita	little house
abuela	grandmother	abuelita	grandma (grammie)
gato	cat	gatito	cute little cat

Note. If a noun ends in **-n**, **-s**, or **-e**, the variation **-cito/a** is added.

café	coffee	cafecito	small coffee
ratón	mouse	ratoncito	little mouse

Exercise C. Form diminutives for the following nouns.

1. hermano   _____
2. plato   _____
3. muchacha   _____
4. coche   _____
5. gata   _____

Augmentatives

While diminutives are common in Spanish and you need to know how to use them, augmentatives are rather rare, and you do not need them at this point. Their inclusion here is really for fun. You must be careful using augmentatives because some of the endings are derogatory.

Rules

1. **-ón.** (Usually augmentative, but may indicate the opposite of the original word.)

el hombre	man	el hombrón	hefty man
el pelo	hair	el pelón	someone who's nearly bald
la silla	chair	el sillón	armchair

Note. At times the gender may change in the augmented version (la silla, el sillón).

2. **-azo.** (A blow by the object indicated or having to do with the object given.)

botella	bottle	botellazo	blow with a bottle
codo	elbow	codazo	nudge (with elbow)
teléfono	phone	telefonazo	phone call

3. **-ote.** (Full of indicated word, positive tone.)

animal	animal	animalote	a bit brutish, but amusing

4. **-ucho.** (Generally negative, though may be positive in a few cases.)

animalucho	repulsive animal
librucho	a bad novel
feucho	ugly, but indicates affection

5. **-ote, ota.** (Negative tone.)

feote	very ugly
palabrota	swearword

Exercise D.

Across Clues	Down Clues
1. uncle	1. record player
2. brother	3. book
4. kitchen	5. picture
5. girl	7. tree
6. cat	8. car
8. food	9. hand
11. name	10. anchor
12. dog	

SUBJECT PRONOUNS AND PREPOSITIONS

SUBJECT PRONOUNS

Here are all the forms of subject pronouns.

I	yo	we	nosotros (-as, *feminine*)
you (*familiar, singular*)	tú	you (*familiar, plural*)	vosotros (-as, *feminine*)
you (*formal, singular*)	usted	you (*formal, plural*)	ustedes (Uds. Vds.)
he	él	they (*masculine*)	ellos
she	ella	they (*feminine*)	ellas

Notes.

1. **Nosotros, vosotros,** and **ellos** have feminine alternates ending in **-as**.

2. **Usted** may be abbreviated as **Ud.** or **Vd.** The plural form, **ustedes,** may be abbreviated as **Uds.** or **Vds.**

3. The familiar **tú** has an alternate, **vos,** which is used by a small percentage of the Spanish-speaking world, notably in Argentina and parts of Central America. It has its roots in medieval Spanish and has its own set of verb endings.

4. **Tú** versus **usted:** The general rule regarding these two forms is that the familiar, **tú,** is used with children, family members, and close friends. The formal form, **usted,** is used elsewhere. However, the situation may not be so simple; regional and sociological factors influence this usage. A friendly young Spaniard and a young Chicano growing up in Texas might use **tú** with nearly everyone, while a middle-aged Mexican living in the interior might use **tú** only with people under a certain age (25 perhaps) and with family members and close friends. Ask native speakers how they deal with this potentially sticky issue. You will hear a variety of responses.

5. **Vosotros** is a familar plural that is used in Spain only in the areas where the CECEO dialect is used. In the areas of Spain where the

SESEO dialect is used, and in Spanish America, **ustedes** is used for the plural for both familiar and formal.

COMMON PREPOSITIONS		
	a	to, at
	en	in, on, at (with a location)
	de	from, of, about
	con	with
	sin	without
	hasta	until
	por	by, for, through, because of, etc.
	para	by, for, in order to + infinitive
	hacia	toward
	según	according to
	contra	against
	desde	since, from
	entre	between, among

Note. The distinction between **por** and **para** is discussed in Chapter 25.

USING DE TO EXPRESS POSSESSION

The structure used to express possession in Spanish is not parallel to the English structure.

el libro de Juan	John's book
la casa de María	Mary's house
el hijo de la doctora	the doctor's son

Rule. In Spanish, **de** is used to express possession. Thus, the equivalent of apostrophe plus the letter "s" in English is **de** plus the possessor.

Exercise A. Translate.

1. Carmen's father   _____
2. Ricardo's car   _____
3. Anita's sister   _____
4. the sister's cat   _____
5. the girl's dog   _____

THE CONTRACTIONS AL AND DEL

Al — to the, at the

There are only two contractions in Spanish and they are both obligatory, not optional as English contractions are.

Ella va al museo.	She goes to the museum.
Él da leche al bebé.	He gives milk to the baby.

Rule. The preposition **a** is combined with the article **el** to form the contraction **al**. The preposition **a** does not form a contraction with any other article.

Ella va a la escuela.	She goes to school.
Él da fruta a los niños.	He gives fruit to the children.

Del — from the, of the, about the

Reinaldo es del campo.	Reinaldo is from the country.
Hablo del pueblo.	I'm talking about the village.
Es del libro.	It is from the book.

Rule. The preposition **de** combines with the article **el** to form the contraction **del**. **De** does not combine with any other article.

Ellos son de los pueblos.	They are from the villages.
Hablo de los caballos.	I'm talking about the horses.

Exercise B. Translate the following:

1. from the mountains   _____
2. from the man   _____
3. to the car   _____
4. about the books   _____
5. to the city   _____

QUESTION WORDS AND BRIEF DIALOGS

**COMMON
QUESTION WORDS**

¿Qué?	What?
¿Cuál?	Which/What?
¿Quién?	Who?
¿Cómo?	How?
¿Dónde?	Where?
¿Cuándo?	When?
¿Cuánto?	How much?
¿Cuántos?	How many?
¿Por qué?	Why?
¿Para qué?	What for?

Learning the question words now will lighten your work load once you begin the verbs in Chapter 6. You will need a working knowledge of the verbs in order to make up your own questions. But for now, practice the following simple, yet practical, questions with a friend. Or, if you are working alone, read the questions and answers aloud, preferably into a tape recorder. Don't be concerned about understanding structure at this point. The structure will be explained step-by-step as you work your way through the chapters.

DIALOGS

Diálogo A

Una Presentación

Juan: Hola, me llamo Juan. ¿Cómo se llama usted?

María: Me llamo María. Mucho gusto.

Juan: El gusto es mío, María. ¿De dónde es usted?

María: Soy de Albuquerque. ¿Y usted?

Juan: Soy de Nueva York, pero vivo en Chicago. ¿Dónde vive usted?

An Introduction

Hi, my name is John. What is your name?

My name's Mary. Glad to meet you.

The pleasure's mine, Mary. Where are you from?

I'm from Albuquerque. And you?

I'm from New York, but I live in Chicago. Where do you live?

17

María: Vivo en Chicago también.

I live in Chicago, too.

Note. The most common way to ask someone's name in Spanish is literally translated into English as "How do you call yourself?"

Diálogo B

En la Clase

Maestra: ¿Qué es esto, niños?

Niños: Es un basurero.

Maestra: Correcto. ¿Para qué es?

Niños: Es para la basura.

Maestra: ¿Cómo es?

Niños: Es grande y gris.

In Class

What is this, children?

It's a trash can.

Right. What's it for?

It's for trash.

What's it like?
(How is it?)

It's big and gray.

Diálogo C

En el Mercado

Vendedor: ¿Cuántos quiere usted, señor?

Señor: Quiero seis, por favor.

Vendedor: Está bien.

Señor: ¿Cuánto es?

Vendedor: Ochenta pesetas, por favor.

In the Market

How many do you want, sir?

I want six, please.

That's fine.

How much is it?

Eighty pesetas, please.

Diálogo D

En la Casa de Conchita

Susana: ¿Quién es ella?

Conchita: Es mi hermana.

Susana: ¿Por qué no vive aquí?

Conchita: Va a la universidad en Boston.

At Shelly's House

Who is she?

She's my sister.

Why doesn't she live here?

She's going to the university in Boston.

Diálogo E

En la Estación

Pedro: ¿Cuándo sale el tren para Los Angeles?

Dependiente: En veinte minutos.

Pedro: Gracias, señor.

In the Station

When does the train leave for Los Angeles?

In twenty minutes.

Thank you, sir.

Exercise A. Fill in the blank with the question word indicated.

Model: ¿_____ libros quiere usted? How many books do you want?
¿Cuántos libros quiere usted?

1. ¿_____ vive usted? Where do you live?

2. ¿_____ es él? Who is he?

3. ¿_____ es esto? What is this?

4. ¿_____ está usted? How are you?

5. ¿_____ es? What's it for?

6. ¿_____ vive usted en Chicago? Why do you live in Chicago?

7. ¿_____ es? How much is it?

8. ¿_____ quiere usted? How many do you want?

9. ¿_____ es tu libro? Which (one) is your book?

10. ¿_____ va usted a México? When are you going to Mexico?

SPECIAL CASES: CÓMO AND CUÁL

In English, when we don't completely hear what a person has just said, we frequently ask, "What?" Don't translate that directly into Spanish. Instead, when you aren't quite certain what was said, reply with, "¿Cómo?" The Spanish speaker will then repeat what he or she just said.

Cuál has a broader usage than does "which" in English. It is used with the verb **ser** to refer to one of a number of items. Study the following examples:

¿Cuál es tu nombre?	What's your name?
¿Cuál es tu número de teléfono?	What's your phone number?

In a strict sense, if the question "¿Qué es tu nombre?" were asked, the answer might be, "It's a label that was given to me when I was born." In a like manner, the question, "¿Qué es tu número de teléfono?" might be answered with, "It's the number you have to dial to reach my house." The implication, then, is that when you use the word **cuál** instead of **qué**, the Spanish speaker knows that you mean "which" of the many possible names or phone numbers belongs to him or her.

ADJECTIVES

Unlike English adjectives, Spanish adjectives must agree in gender (masculine or feminine) and in number (singular or plural) with the nouns they modify. Descriptive adjectives generally follow the noun. Adjectives that express quantity or possession usually precede the noun.

DESCRIPTIVE ADJECTIVES

In the following examples, the adjectives "white" and "small" reflect the gender of the nouns they modify.

Adjectives Ending in -o

La casa blanca es pequeña.	The white house is small.
El edificio blanco es pequeño.	The white building is small.
Las casas blancas son pequeñas.	The white houses are small.
Los edificios blancos son pequeños.	The white buildings are small.

Rule. Adjectives that end in -o are changed to -a to modify a feminine noun. If the noun is plural, make the adjective plural by adding an -s.

Common Adjectives Ending in -o

alto	tall	gordo	fat
amarillo	yellow	guapo	good looking
barato	inexpensive	hermoso	beautiful
bonito	pretty	limpio	clean
bueno	good	malo	bad
cansado	tired	moderno	modern
caro	expensive	morado	purple
cómodo	comfortable	negro	black
corto	short	nervioso	nervous
delgado	thin	pequeño	small
duro	hard	rico	rich
enfermo	sick	rojo	red

extranjero	foreigner	sucio	dirty
feo	ugly	viejo	old
frío	cold	vivo	alive, lively

Exercise A. Translate the adjectives in parentheses into Spanish.

Model: La casa es _____ (white).
La casa es blanca.

1. Las casas son _____ (red) y _____ (yellow).
2. La cocina es _____ (small).
3. Es una casa _____ (modern).
4. Las calles (streets) son _____ (long).
5. ¿Quiénes son los hombres _____ (foreign)?
6. Las chicas son _____ (thin).
7. Las canciones en español son muy _____ (pretty).
8. Los chicos están _____ (nervous) antes del examen.
9. Es un coche _____ (expensive).
10. Las sillas _____ (comfortable) están en la sala.

Adjectives that End in -e or a Consonant

Adjectives that end in **-e** or a consonant (except for adjectives of nationality and a few that are based on verbs) have the same form for both masculine and feminine.

La mesa es verde.	The table is green.
Los coches son verdes también.	The cars are green also.
La leccion es fácil.	The lesson is easy.
El ejercicio es difícil.	The exercise is difficult.
Los ejercicios son difíciles.	The exercises are difficult.

Rule. Adjectives that end in **-e** or a consonant have the same form for both masculine and feminine. To make these adjectives plural, add an **-s** to a final **-e**, and **-es** to a consonant. If the singular form has an accent mark on the last syllable, that accent mark is dropped in the plural form.

Common Adjectives that End in -e

elegante	elegant
fuerte	strong
grande	large
inteligente	intelligent
impresionante	impressive
pobre	poor
triste	sad
verde	green

Common Adjectives that End in a Consonant

azul	blue
difícil	difficult
fácil	easy
feliz	happy
gris	gray
joven	young
militar	military
nacional	national
natal	native
popular	popular

Exercise B. Write the correct form of the adjective in parentheses and translate the phrase into English.

Model: una niña (bueno)

una niña buena   a good girl

1. unas lecciones (fácil) _____
2. dos corbatas (ties) (gris) _____
3. una mujer (fuerte) _____
4. los examenes (difícil) _____
5. los chicos (pobre) _____

Exercise C. Change the phrase to the plural.

Model: la casa blanca
las casas blancas

1. el baile (dance) nacional _____
2. la niña feliz _____
3. el chico joven _____
4. el profesor impresionante _____
5. la pluma azul _____

Adjectives of Nationality

Adjectives of nationality that end in -o follow the rules already given for other adjectives ending in -o. Adjectives of nationality that end in a consonant, however, follow a pattern that differs from the rule for other adjectives ending in a consonant. Note the following examples:

El hombre español	La mujer española
Los hombres españoles	Las mujeres españolas

Rule. When the masculine form of an adjective of nationality ends in a consonant, the feminine form ends in -a. Adjectives of nationality are not capitalized.

Some Adjectives of Nationality

alemán	German	holandés	Dutch
árabe	Arabic	inglés	English
argentino	Argentinean	irlandés	Irish
brasileño	Brazilian	italiano	Italian
chileno	Chilean	japonés	Japanese
chino	Chinese	mexicano	Mexican
colombiano	Columbian	peruano	Peruvian
español	Spanish	ruso	Russian
francés	French	sueco	Swedish
griego	Greek	suizo	Swiss
guatemalteco	Guatemalan	venezolano	Venezuelan

Exercise D. Rewrite the following sentences using the words in parentheses.

Model: Mi primo es griego. (Mis primos)

        Mis primos son griegos.

1. El actor es francés. (Los actores)

    _____

2. El sombrero es español. (Los sombreros)

    _____

3. Juana es alemana. (Juan)

    _____

4. El hombre es inglés. (Los hombres)

    _____

5. Mis abuelos son irlandeses. (Mi abuela)

    _____

Exercise E. Complete the following sentences with the correct form of the adjective in parentheses.

Model: La comida es _____ (Chinese).

        La comida es china.

1. Ana es _____ (Italian).
2. Las cestas (baskets) son _____ (Mexican).
3. La manta (blanket) es _____ (Peruvian).
4. Los coches son _____ (German).
5. Mi abuela es _____ (Dutch).

Adjectives Generated from Verbs: -dor, -dora

Some adjectives follow the same rules as the adjectives of nationality. Though there are only a few, they are worth mentioning. They tend to come from active verbs and modify animate objects.

copiador/copiadora (copiar)	copying
encantador/encantadora (encantar)	charming
hablador/habladora (hablar)	talkative, gossipy
fatigador/fatigadora (fatigar)	tiring, annoying
labrador/labradora (labrar)	industrious
ladrador/ladradora (ladrar)	barking
trabajador/trabajadora (trabajar)	hard-working

Examples.

Ella es una mujer encantadora.	She is a charming woman.
Juan es muy trabajador.	Juan is very hard-working.
Emilia es habladora.	Emily is talkative.

QUANTITATIVE ADJECTIVES

Notice in the following examples that the descriptive adjectives precede the nouns they modify. They also agree in number (singular/plural) and gender with the nouns they modify (some, however, have the same form for masculine and feminine).

Hay mucha gente en la Ciudad de México.	There are a lot of people in Mexico City.
Mi perro tiene pocas pulgas.	My dog has few fleas.
Hay demasiado azúcar en este cereal.	There's too much sugar in this cereal.
No hay bastantes sillas.	There aren't enough chairs.
Ella tiene tantas amigas.	She has so many friends.

Common Quantitative Adjectives

mucho/a	a lot, many
poco/a	few
demasiado/a	too much; plural, too many
bastante	enough
suficiente	sufficient, enough
tanto/a	so much
tantos/as	so many

Rule. Adjectives indicating quantity precede the nouns they modify. Rules for agreement are the same as those for descriptive adjectives. Numbers also precede nouns. (See Chapter 8 for details.)

Exercise F. Translate the adjective in parentheses.

Model: Juan tiene (has) _____ (many) amigos en México.

Juan tiene muchos amigos en México.

1. Ella come (eats) _____ (too many) dulces durante las vacaciones.

2. Él no tiene _____ (enough) dinero.

3. ¿Qué hace Ud. (do you do) con _____ (so much) dinero?

4. ¿Dónde pone Ud. (do you put) _____ (so many) flores?

5. Tenemos muy _____ (little) tiempo.

6. Hay (there are) _____ (few) tigres en México.

POSSESSIVE ADJECTIVES

Subject Pronoun	Possessive Adjective	Translation
yo	mi/mis	my
tú	tu/tus	your
usted	su/sus	your
él	su/sus	his
ella	su/sus	her
nosotros	nuestro (m.)/nuestros nuestra (f.)/nuestras	our
vosotros	vuestro (m.)/vuestros vuestra (f.)/vuestras	your
ustedes	su/sus	your
ellos	su/sus	their
ellas	su/sus	their

Examples.

Es mi libro.	It is my book.
Son nuestros libros.	They are our books.
Ella tiene su libro.	She has her book.
¿Dónde están vuestros libros?	Where are your books?

Note. As you see, the possessives **su** and **sus** might be ambiguous. Since either word could be translated "your," "his," "her," or "their," you might need to clarify the meaning by using the following forms.

su libro	your book (sing.)	el libro de usted
	his book	el libro de él
	her book	el libro de ella
	your book (pl.)	el libro de ustedes
	their book	el libro de ellos/ellas

Rules.

1. The possessive adjective, used to indicate ownership, is singular if the noun it modifies is singular. It is plural if the noun it modifies is plural.

2. **Nuestro** and **vuestro** are the only two possessive adjectives that have both masculine and feminine forms.

3. If the meaning of **su** or **sus** appears ambiguous, you may clarify the meaning by using **de** plus the subject pronoun or a proper noun. For example, **su libro** could mean **el libro de él** or **el libro de ustedes**. Or, **sus casas** could be changed to **las casas de ellos** or **las casas de ustedes**.

4. The possessive adjective is generally replaced by the definite article when referring to parts of the body and articles of clothing. This is particularly true with reflexive verbs. See Chapter 13 on reflexive verbs for more examples.

Example.

Me lavo las manos.	I wash my hands.
Ella se pone los zapatos.	She puts on her shoes.

Exercise G. Write the correct possessive adjective.

1. Juan prepara _____ (his) lección todos los días.
2. Tú tienes _____ (your) pluma.
3. Yo tengo el dinero en _____ (my) cartera (wallet).
4. Teresita está con _____ (her) abuelos.
5. ¿Dónde está _____ (your) pasaporte, Señor Gómez?
6. Los Olivares están en _____ (their) casa.
7. Vosotros habláis con _____ (your) profesora.
8. Nosotros visitamos a _____ (our) primos.
9. Tú estás en España con _____ (your) padres.
10. Ellos están con _____ (their) hermanas.

Exercise H. Translate the words given in parentheses.

1. (Their family) está en Tijuana.   _____
2. (Our school) no es muy grande.   _____
3. (My friends) son ricos.   _____
4. (His father) está en el centro.   _____
5. (Her photos) son muy bonitas.   _____

Exercise C.

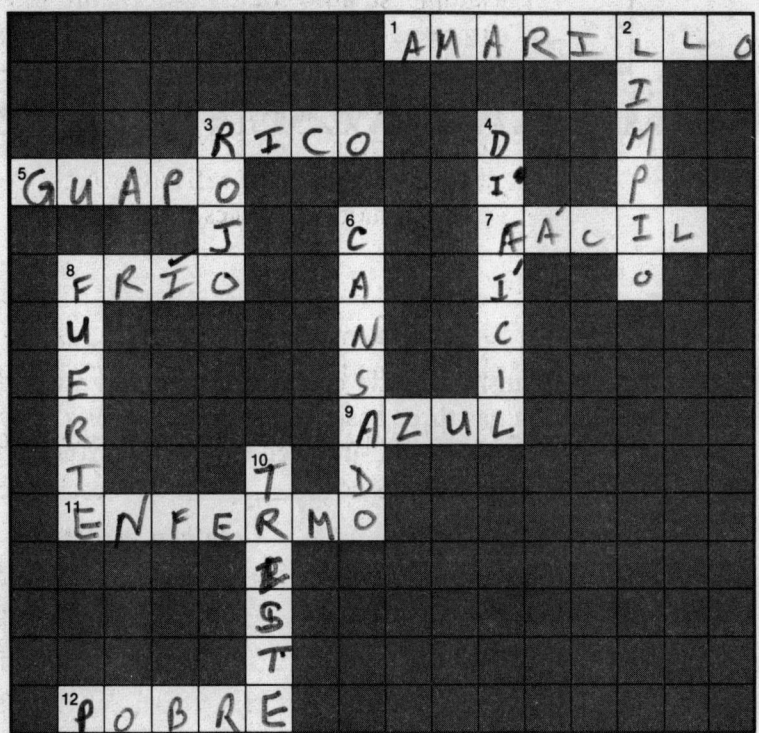

Across Clues

1. yellow
3. rich
5. handsome
7. easy
8. cold
9. blue
11. sick
12. poor

Down Clues

2. clean
3. red
4. difficult
6. tired
8. strong
10. sad

REGULAR PRESENT TENSE VERBS

An English infinitive consists of "to" plus a verb (to run, to go, and so on). Spanish has three basic verb types, categorized by the vowel in the infinitive form: **-ar, -er,** and **-ir.** Each type will be studied in this chapter.

-AR OR FIRST CONJUGATION VERBS

Common -ar Verbs

ayudar	to help	llevar	to take, carry, wear
bailar	to dance	mandar	to send, order
cambiar	to change	mirar	to look
cantar	to sing	necesitar	to need
comprar	to buy	pagar	to pay
dejar	to leave, allow	pasar	to pass, happen
desear	to wish	preguntar	to ask
enseñar	to teach, show	preparar	to prepare
esperar	to hope, wait, expect	regresar	to return
estudiar	to study	escuchar	to listen
ganar	to win, earn	tomar	to take, have (food/drink)
hablar	to talk/speak	trabajar	to work
invitar	to invite	usar	to use
lavar	to wash	viajar	to travel
llamar	to call	visitar	to visit

Rule. To conjugate a verb in the present tense, take off the **-ar** ending of the infinitive and add the appropriate subject pronoun ending to the stem.

-ar Verb Endings

Person	Singular		Plural	
1st	(yo)	-o	(nosotros)	-amos
2nd	(tú)	-as	(vosotros)	-áis
3rd	(usted)	-a	(ustedes, Uds.)	-an
	(él	-a	(ellos)	-an
	(ella)	-a	(ellas)	-an

Examples.

yo: bailo, canto, deseo, espero, hablo, pregunto, trabajo

tú: ayudas, compras, dejas, enseñas, esperas, preguntas

usted: cambia, gana, habla, invita, lava, mira, prepara

él: baila, llama, lleva, necesita, pasa, toma, viaja

ella: desea, habla, manda, paga, regresa, trabaja

nosotros: ayudamos, dejamos, lavamos, pasamos, usamos

vosotros: compráis, esperáis, habláis, miráis, pasáis, tomáis

ustedes: dejan, esperan, ganan, miran, necesitan

ellos: cantan, llaman, llevan, preparan, toman, visitan

ellas: bailan, enseñan, mandan, regresan, viajan

Translation of the Present Tense

In most cases, the Spanish present tense is translated as the simple present tense in English. For example:

Ella habla inglés.	She speaks English.
Él canta mal.	He sings badly.
Yo pregunto el precio.	I ask the price.
Ella prepara la comida.	She prepares the food.
Nosotros pasamos dos días en San Francisco.	We spend two days in San Francisco.
Mandamos el dinero a Felipe.	We send the money to Felipe.

The present tense in Spanish may also be translated into English as a present progressive.

Examples.

¿Qué pasa?	What's happening?
Ellos trabajan hoy.	They are working today.

Note. There is a present progressive tense in Spanish (see Chapter 11), but it is generally used only to emphasize an action in progress.

Examples.

Está lloviendo.	It's raining.
Estamos estudiando.	We are studying.

Omission of Subject Pronoun

When the subject of a verb is understood, it may be omitted. This is common practice with verb forms whose endings make the subject clear (yo, tú, vosotros, nosotros).

Examples.

Como en la cafetería.	I eat in the cafeteria.
Regresamos mañana.	We return tomorrow.

Exercise A. Change the verb to agree with the new subject.

Model: Ella trabaja mucho. Yo _____
        Yo trabajo.

1. Ella lava el perro.   Tú _____
2. Usted ayuda en casa.   Ellos _____
3. Juan llama por teléfono.   Yo _____
4. Nosotros compramos fruta.   Vosotros _____
5. El invita a María.   Nosotros _____
6. Yo pregunto su nombre.   Ustedes _____
7. La familia regresa.   Tú _____
8. Carmen baila muy bien.   Él _____
9. Usted enseña la historia.   Ella _____
10. Ellos regresan mañana.   Yo _____

Exercise B. Fill the blank with the appropriate verb on the right.

Model: Mi amigo _____ café con leche.
        Mi amigo toma café con leche.

1. Los estudiantes _____ mucho.   a. mandamos
2. Tomás _____ la lección.   b. necesito
3. Yo _____ preparar la comida.   c. bailamos
4. Margarita y yo _____ la rumba.   d. prepara
5. Ustedes _____ en italiano.   e. gana
6. Marta _____ mucho dinero.   f. cantan
7. Nosotros _____ la televisión.   g. estudian
8. Javier _____ muchos libros.   h. viajan
9. Elena y Luis _____ en México.   i. compra
10. Nosotros _____ una carta a Lola.   j. miramos

Exercise C. Fill in the blank with the correct form of the verb indicated.

Model: Ellas _____ el tren. (take)
        Ellas toman el tren.

1. Tú _____ el paquete. (send)
2. Yo _____ mi dinero en el banco. (exchange)
3. Ella _____ en el hospital. (works)
4. Ustedes _____ la música. (listen)

5. Pepe _____ la lotería. (wins)

6. Ellos _____ a Chicago. (travel)

7. Carolina y yo _____ tarde. (return)

8. Tú _____ poco tiempo aquí. (spend)

9. El _____ una casa. (buys)

10. Nosotros _____ en el club. (dance)

MAKING QUESTIONS AND NEGATIVES

Examples.

¿Baila usted los sábados?	Do you dance on Saturdays?
Diego no toma vino.	Diego doesn't drink wine.
¿Ayudas tú en la cocina?	Do you help in the kitchen?
Pedro no habla mucho chino.	Pedro doesn't speak much Chinese.
¿No trabaja Julián?	Doesn't Julian work?

Rules.

1. To make a question, place the subject after the verb.

Statement:	Usted habla mucho.	You talk a lot.
Question:	¿Habla usted mucho?	Do you talk a lot?

2. To make a sentence negative, simply place the word "no" in front of the verb.

Affirmative:	José canta bien.	Jose sings well.
Negative:	José no canta bien.	Jose doesn't sing well.

3. To form a question when the subject is long (two or more words), take the entire subject and place it at the end.

Statement:	Los estudiantes buenos estudian mucho.	Good students study a lot.
Question:	¿Estudian mucho los estudiantes buenos?	Do good students study a lot?

4. If the subject of a statement is not expressed, then the word order will remain the same in a question. When speaking, simply change your voice inflection. Practice the following similar change in English.

Statement:	John's here.
Question:	John's here? (As though you are surprised.)

Now try some changes in intonation pattern in Spanish.

Statement:	Deseamos el café ahora.	We wish coffee now.
Question:	¿Deseamos el café ahora?	Do we wish coffee now?
Statement:	Trabajo mañana.	I work tomorrow.
Question:	¿Trabajo mañana.	Do I work tomorrow?

5. Place "no" before the verb in the question to make a negative question.

Example.

¿No trabaja Ud.?   Don't you work?

Exercise D. Answer the following questions affirmatively or negatively as indicated. If the question is asked in the singular (**Ud., tú**), answer in the **yo** form. If it is asked in the plural (**Uds., vosotros**), answer in the **nosotros** form.

Models: ¿Necesita Ud. el libro?   Sí, necesito el libro.

¿Pagan Uds. mucho?   No, no pagamos mucho.

1. ¿Mira Ud. el programa? Sí,

   _____

2. ¿Enseñan Uds. la geografía? No, no

   _____

3. ¿Desean Uds. más café? Sí,

   _____

4. ¿Compras tú muchos discos? No, no

   _____

5. ¿Preparáis vosotros la comida? Sí,

   _____

6. ¿Canta Ud. bien? Sí,

   _____

7. ¿Regresan Uds. mañana? Sí,

   _____

8. ¿Viaja Ud. en octubre? No, no

   _____

9. ¿Dejan Uds. una propina (tip)? Sí,

   _____

10. ¿Necesitan Uds. agua? Sí,

   _____

DIÁLOGO   **En La Fiesta**

(Read aloud.)

José y Patricia llegan a la casa de Julia. Julia contesta la puerta.

Julia: Hola, José y Patricia. ¿Cómo están?

José y Patricia: Bien, gracias. ¿Y tú?

Julia: Muy bien.

Ellos pasan a la sala donde ocho jóvenes escuchan discos y hablan y toman refrescos.

José: Hola, amigos. ¿Qué tal? ¿Qué escuchan?

Manolo: Escuchamos una canción de Claudia de Colombia. Ella canta muy bien.

José: Sí, es una canción bonita. ¿Bailamos, Patricia?

Patricia: Sí, cómo no.

José: Tú bailas muy bien.

Patricia: Tú bailas bien, también. ¿Dónde trabajas ahora?

José: Todavía trabajo en la zapatería, pero pocas horas porque estudio mucho.

Patricia: ¿Qué estudias ahora?

José: Estudio química, biología, historia, matemáticas aplicadas y francés. ¿Hablas francés?

Patricia: Un poco. Necesito estudiar más.

Exercise E. Preguntas sobre el diálogo (questions on the dialog).

1. ¿Dónde están José y Patricia?

   _____

2. ¿Quién contesta la puerta?

   _____

3. ¿Quiénes escuchan discos?

   _____

4. ¿Qué toman?

   _____

5. ¿Dónde trabaja José?

   _____

6. ¿Por qué trabaja pocas horas?

   _____

7. ¿Qué estudia José?

   _____

8. ¿Habla francés Patricia?

   _____

PERSONAL "A"   Spanish has a unique grammatical marker that English does not have. The word **a** is used after a verb that is followed by an object referring to a person. This **a** is not translated. It does have meaning, however. It tells us that what follows the verb is a person. It may be used with animals or place names as well. It is used with all verbs except **tener** (to have).

Veo a mi amigo.   I see my friend.

but: Veo mi casa.   I see my house.

Llevo a mi hermano.   I take my brother.

but: Llevo mi libro.   I take my book.

Exercise F. Translate the following:

1. I help my father. _____

2. They invite David. _____

3. We visit Beatriz. _____

4. He teaches Pedro. _____

5. She asks Juan. _____

-ER OR SECOND CONJUGATION VERBS

Common -er Verbs

aprender	to learn	esconder	to hide
beber	to drink	leer	to read
comer	to eat	meter	to put
comprender	to understand	prometer	to promise
correr	to run	responder	to respond
creer	to believe, think	romper	to break
deber	to owe, ought to	vender	to sell

Rule. To conjugate a verb in the present tense, take the -er ending off the infinitive and add the appropriate subject pronoun ending to the stem.

-er Verb Endings

Person	Singular		Plural	
1st	(yo)	-o	(nosotros)	-emos
2nd	(tú)	-es	(vosotros)	-éis
3rd	(usted)	-e	(ustedes)	-en
	(él	-e	(ellos)	-en
	(ella)	-e	(ellas)	-en

Examples.

yo: aprendo, bebo, como, escondo, leo, meto

tú: aprendes, corres, debes, prometes, respondes, rompes

usted: aprende, corre, come, esconde, mete, vende

él: bebe, debe, lee, promete, responde, lee

ella: aprende, come, esconde, corre, mete, rompe

vosotros: bebéis, coméis, escondéis, leéis, metéis

ustedes: aprenden, corren, comen, esconden, meten

ellos/ellas: beben, comen, prometen, responden, venden

nosotros: aprendemos, corremos, comemos, metemos, vendemos

Exercise G. Change the verb to agree with the new subject.

Model: Ella aprende mucho. Nosotros _____ mucho.
Nosotros aprendemos mucho.

1. Ella responde en español.   Tú _____
2. Yo corro en la playa.   Él _____
3. Nosotros aprendemos el italiano.   Usted _____
4. Roberto vende la casa.   Ellos _____
5. Vosotros leéis el periódico.   Nosotros _____
6. Tú bebes jugo.   Vosotros _____
7. Tú y yo comemos en el restaurante.   Ella _____
8. Mi hermano promete comer con ella.   Tú _____
9. La familia García vende el coche.   Yo _____
10. El niño rompe el vaso.   Él _____

Exercise H. Fill in the blank with the correct form of the verb indicated.

Model: Julián _____ su bicicleta. (breaks)
Julián rompe su bicicleta.

1. Juan Antonio _____ mucho dinero. (owes)
2. Margarita _____ vino blanco con la comida. (drinks)
3. El perro _____ el hueso (bone). (hides)
4. Tomás _____ dos millas diariamente (daily). (runs)
5. Yo no _____ el japonés. (understand)
6. Paco _____ su bicicleta. (sells)
7. Vosotros no _____ mucho. (eat)
8. Nosotros _____ la comida en el refrigerador. (put)
9. Ellos _____ la novela. (read)
10. Tomás _____ aprender la lección. (promises)

Exercise I. Answer the following questions in the affirmative. Translate your answer.

Model: ¿Qué beben ustedes?
Nosotros bebemos jugo. We drink juice.

1. ¿Lee usted mucho?

   _____

   _____

2. ¿Qué come usted en su restaurante favorito?

   _____

   _____

3. ¿Compreden ustedes el español?

_____

_____

4. ¿Responden ustedes en español en la clase?

_____

_____

5. ¿Corre usted diariamente?

_____

_____

6. ¿Rompe usted muchas cosas (things)?

_____

_____

7. ¿Venden ustedes la casa?

_____

_____

8. ¿Debe usted dinero a su padre?

_____

_____

-IR OR THIRD CONJUGATION VERBS

Common -ir Verbs

abrir	to open	escribir	to write
admitir	to admit	recibir	to receive
asistir	to attend	subir	to go up, raise, climb
decidir	to decide	vivir	to live

Rule. To conjugate these verbs in the present tense, take off the -ir ending of the infinitive and add the appropriate subject pronoun ending to the stem.

-ir Verb Endings

Person	Singular		Plural	
1st	(yo)	-o	(nosotros)	-imos
2nd	(tú)	-es	(vosotros)	-ís
3rd	(usted)	-e	(ustedes)	-en
	(él)	-e	(ellos)	-en
	(ella)	-e	(ellas)	-en

Note. The endings for -er and -ir verbs are identical except for the nosotros and vosotros forms.

Exercise J. Fill in the blank with the correct form of the infinitive.

Model: Yo _____ en Chicago. (vivir)

Yo vivo en Chicago.

REGULAR PRESENT TENSE VERBS **37**

1. Ella _____ muchas cartas (letters). (escribir)
2. Vicente _____ la puerta (door). (abrir)
3. Nosotros _____ la montaña. (subir)
4. Tú _____ a la clase. (asistir)
5. Ellos _____ pronto. (decidir)

Exercise K. Fill in the blank with the correct form of the verb indicated.

Model: Ustedes _____ en Austin. (live)
   Ustedes viven en Austin.

1. Ana Hernandez _____ muchas cartas. (writes)
2. Yo _____ muchas cuentas (bills). (receive)
3. Vosotros _____ a la fiesta. (attend)
4. Tú no _____ la verdad (truth). (admit)
5. Ellos _____ los libros. (open)
6. Nosotros _____. (decide)
7. Usted _____ en una ciudad bonita. (live)
8. Él _____ a su apartamento. (goes up)

Exercise L. Answer the following questions affirmatively. Translate your answers.

Model: ¿Dónde vive usted?
   Yo vivo en Buffalo. I live in Buffalo.

1. ¿Abre usted el libro en la clase?

   _____

   _____

2. ¿A qué escuela asiste usted?

   _____

   _____

3. ¿Vive usted cerca (near) de la escuela?

   _____

   _____

4. ¿Qué escribe usted?

   _____

   _____

5. ¿Admite usted sus errores?

   _____

   _____

6. ¿Recibe usted muchas cartas?

   _____

   _____

DIÁLOGO

Marta y Mario

(Read aloud.)

Marta y su hermano hablan en la cocina.

Mario: Marta, siempre escondes mis llaves.

Marta: Ay, Mario, ¿por qué no miras en la mesa? Están allí.

Mario: Gracias. ¿Comemos tarde hoy?

Marta: No, temprano. Papá necesita regresar a la oficina.

Mario: Entonces, ¿no corremos juntos en la playa?

Marta: Hoy no, pero Papá promete correr con nosotros mañana.

Mario: Muy bien. ¿Qué lees en el periódico?

Marta: Un artículo sobre las Naciones Unidas. ¿Crees tú que Libia debe romper con las Naciones Unidas?

Mario: En realidad no comprendo la situación. ¿Comprendes tú?

Marta: No muy bien. Debo leer más para aprender más.

Exercise M. Preguntas sobre el diálogo.

1. ¿Quiénes hablan en la cocina?

   _____

2. ¿Dónde están las llaves de Mario?

   _____

3. ¿Quién necesita regresar a la oficina?

   _____

4. ¿Dónde corren Marta y Mario con su papá?

   _____

5. ¿Qué lee Marta en el periódico?

   _____

SER/ESTAR AND HAY

SER/ESTAR: Both **ser** and **estar** mean "to be," but they are not interchangeable. **Estar** is
TO BE used to describe a temporary condition and to give a location, whether temporary or permanent. **Ser** is used to express an inherent quality, profession, nationality, place of origin, appearance, ownership, substance of which a thing is made, times, dates, and seasons. It is also used with predicate nouns or pronouns and in impersonal expressions.

Person		Estar	Ser
1st	(yo)	estoy	soy
2nd	(tú)	estás	eres
3rd	(Ud., él, ella)	está	es
1st	(nosotros, -as)	estamos	somos
2nd	(vosotros, -as)	estáis	sois
3rd	(Uds., ellos, -as)	están	son

Estar

Location

El gato está en la casa.   The cat is in the house.

Houston está en Texas.   Houston is in Texas.

¿Dónde está Juan?   Where is John?

Temporary Condition

Mi tía está cansada.   My aunt is tired.

El café está frío.   The coffee is cold.

La puerta está cerrada.   The door is closed.

El hombre está enfermo.   The man is sick.

Note. It may be helpful to think of these conditions as the result of an action, or as reversible conditions that alternate with an opposite, or as conditions that could change within a day or two.

An Impression

Juanito está tan alto.   Johnny looks so tall.

Tiene sólo ocho años?   Is he only eight?

José López está viejo.	Jose Lopez looks old. (The poor man looks older than he is.)
Anita, estás muy bonita hoy.	Ann, you look pretty today.

Note. Estar is used to indicate an impression, how we think something appears. The best translation in such cases is "looks."

Exercise A. Fill in the blanks with the correct form of estar.

1. Ella _____ en casa.
2. Los paquetes _____ en la cocina.
3. Tú _____ muy contento hoy.
4. Cuando Pablo _____ en Nueva York, habla inglés.
5. París _____ en Francia.
6. Yo no _____ enfermo.
7. Cuando ustedes _____ enfermos, no trabajan.
8. Nosotros _____ en el restaurante.
9. El libro _____ en la mesa.
10. Ellos _____ cansados hoy.

Ser	El helado es dulce.	Ice cream is sweet.
Inherent Quality or Characteristic	Los limones son agrios.	Lemons are sour.
	Los italianos son románticos.	Italians are romantic.
	Isabel es inteligente.	Isabel is intelligent.
Profession	Diana es escritora.	Diane is a writer.
	Mi primo es abogado.	My cousin is a lawyer.
	Él es un abogado trabajador.	He's a hard-working lawyer.

Note. If the profession is not modified, as in the first two examples, the indefinite article (**una/un**) is omitted.

Nationality	Tomás es español.	Thomas is Spanish.
	Ellos son mexicanos.	They are Mexican.
	Graciela es cubana.	Graciela is Cuban.
Place of Origin	Mariana es de Barcelona.	Marian is from Barcelona.
	Armando es de Caracas.	Armando is from Caracas.
Appearance	Carlos es guapo.	Carl is handsome.
	Julieta es bonita.	Julie is pretty.
Ownership	El libro es de Pedro.	The book is Peter's.
	La pluma es mía.	The pen is mine.
	El coche es de Susana.	The car is Susan's.
Substance	La mesa es de madera.	The table is wooden.
	El anillo es de plata.	The ring is silver.

	Los aretes son de oro.	The earrings are gold.
Times, Days, Dates, Months, Seasons	¿Qué hora es?	What time is it?
	Son las dos.	It's two o'clock.
	Hoy es viernes el quince.	Today is Friday the 15th.
	Es el mes de junio.	It is the month of June.
To Express a Predicate Noun or Pronoun	Ese hombre es Jaime García.	That man is Jaime Garcia.
	Patricia es mi hermana.	Patricia is my sister.
	Yo soy Jaime Martinez.	I am Jaime Martinez.
Impersonal Expressions	Es importante.	It is important.
	No es necesario.	It isn't necessary.
	Es dudable.	It is doubtful.

Exercise B. Fill in the form with the correct form of ser.

1. La casa _____ blanca.
2. Tú _____ de Venezuela, ¿no?
3. Ellos _____ estudiantes.
4. Yo _____ una persona generosa.
5. El _____ médico.
6. Usted _____ muy amable.
7. Mi perro _____ inteligente.
8. Ustedes _____ mexicanos, ¿no?
9. Nosotros _____ amigos.
10. Ella _____ la hermana de Rosa.

Contrasts Between Ser and Estar

1. Remember that **estar** is used when the condition is temporary.

Juan está triste y cansado.	John is sad and tired. (Hopefully, he'll be fine by tomorrow.)
Usted está tan ocupado.	You are so busy.

2. Some conditions may seem to have a quality of temporariness, but **ser** is used because that quality is not going to change in a day or two.

El coche es nuevo.	The car is new.
Usted es joven.	You are young.

Note the following contrasting sentences:

Las uvas son verdes.	The grapes are green. (Not purple.)
Las uvas están verdes.	The grapes are green. (Not ripe yet.)
Los tacos son buenos en ese restaurante.	The tacos are good in that restaurant. (Good place!)

Los tacos están buenos hoy.		The tacos are good today.
¿Cómo es tu hermano?		What's your brother like?
¿Cómo está tu hermano?		How's your brother?

3. The meaning of some words depends on whether they are used with **ser** or with **estar**.

	With Estar	**With Ser**
malo	sick	bad
listo	ready	clever
vivo	alive	lively

Note. With words such as **soltero** (bachelor) either **ser** or **estar** may be used. **Soy soltero** means **I am a bachelor** in that I belong to the bachelor group. "Estoy soltero" means "I am still a bachelor."

Special cases: contento, feliz, muerto

Estoy contento.	I am happy.
El gato es feliz.	The cat is happy.
Mi padre está muerto.	My father is dead.

Estar is used with **contento**, but **ser** is used with **feliz**. **Estar** is used with **muerto**.

Exercise C. Answer the following questions affirmatively.

1. ¿Está usted en casa en este momento?

   _____

2. ¿Es usted simpático?

   _____

3. ¿Son ustedes estudiantes excelentes?

   _____

4. ¿Es usted una persona nerviosa?

   _____

5. ¿Está usted nervioso en este momento?

   _____

6. ¿Es usted joven?

   _____

7. ¿Está usted contento?

   _____

8. ¿Están ellas cansadas?

   _____

9. ¿Es rico el señor Rubio?

   _____

10. ¿Es bonita Carolina?

_____

Exercise D. Fill in the correct form of ser or estar.

1. La pluma _____ de José.

2. Ustedes _____ ocupados.

3. Yo _____ de Puerto Rico.

4. Ahora yo _____ en Boston.

5. Nosotros _____ hermanos.

6. La comida _____ fría.

7. Mi amigo _____ español.

8. _____ importante estudiar.

9. La capital de España _____ Madrid.

10. Mi amiga _____ guapa.

DIÁLOGO *Hoy es lunes. Diego está en la clase de inglés. Diego es inteligente y guapo. Carolina está contenta porque Diego se sienta a su lado* (sits down beside her).

Diego: Estás bonita hoy, Carolina.

Carolina: Gracias, Diego.

Diego: ¿Cómo estás?

Carolina: ¿Bien, gracias. ¿Y tú?

Diego: ¿Estás lista para mañana?

Carolina: ¿Qué pasa mañana?

Diego: Mañana es mi cumpleaños.

Carolina: Ay, Diego. Es verdad. Sí, es un día especial.

Diego: Hay un café italiano donde sirven comidas fabulosas. ¿Quieres (do you want) comer conmigo?

Carolina: Sí, gracias.

Exercise E. Translate.

1. We are from California. _____

2. They are very busy. _____

3. Are you (tú) sick today? _____

4. Where is Carlos? _____

5. He is my friend. _____

6. She looks pretty. _____

7. He is very clever. _____

8. Tomorrow is Friday. _____

9. It is important. _____

10. The house is modern. _____

HAY: THERE IS/THERE ARE

The verb **hay** is unusual. It comes from the infinitive **haber,** "to have," but it is not part of the regular conjugation. **Haber** is discussed in Chapter 27 as an auxiliary verb used in forming compound tenses. Right now we want to see how it is used to mean "there is" and "there are."

Examples.

Hay un extranjero guapo en mi clase.	There is a handsome foreigner in my class.
¿Dónde hay un restaurante bueno?	Where is there a good restaurant?

Note. There is a difference between "there are" and "they are":

Hay sillas cómodas.	There are comfortable chairs.
Son sillas cómodas.	They are comfortable chairs.
Hay dos gimnastas en la clase.	There are two gymnasts in the class.
Los dos gimnastas están en la clase.	The two gymnasts are in the class.

Notice, also, the difference between "there is" and "it is":

Hay un libro muy importante.	There is a very important book.
Es un libro muy importante.	It is a very important book.
Hay un lagarto en la cocina.	There's a lizard in the kitchen.
El lagarto está en la cocina.	The lizard is in the kitchen.

Rule. Hay may be followed by either a singular or a plural noun. It is translated either as "there is" or "there are" and is thus not the same as **es/son,** or **está/están.**

Exercise F. Fill in the blank with the correct translation of the verb given in English.

1. _____ un elefante muy grande. (It is)
2. _____ una casa amarilla en mi calle. (There is)
3. _____ mis amigos. (They are)
4. _____ muy cansados. (They are)
5. _____ tiburones (sharks) cerca de la playa? (Are there)
6. _____ aquí? (Are they)
7. _____ estudiantes jóvenes en la clase. (There are)
8. _____ jóvenes, pero _____ muy inteligentes. (They are, they are)
9. _____ una ciudad muy limpia. (It is)
10. _____ muchas ciudades hermosas en España. (There are)

NUMBERS, DAYS, MONTHS, SEASONS

NUMBERS

Cardinal Numbers

1–30

1	uno	11	once	21	veintiuno
2	dos	12	doce	22	veintidós
3	tres	13	trece	23	veintitrés
4	cuatro	14	catorce	24	veinticuatro
5	cinco	15	quince	25	veinticinco
6	seis	16	dieciséis	26	veintiséis
7	siete	17	diecisiete	27	veintisiete
8	ocho	18	dieciocho	28	veintiocho
9	nueve	19	diecinueve	29	veintinueve
10	diez	20	veinte	30	treinta

Note. Numbers 16–19 and 21–29 may also be written as three words. For example, 16 could be diez y seis, and 21 could be veinte y uno.

30–900

31	treinta y uno	100	ciento, cien
40	cuarenta	200	doscientos
42	cuarenta y dos	300	trescientos
50	cincuenta	400	cuatrocientos
53	cincuenta y tres	500	quinientos
60	sesenta	600	seiscientos
64	sesenta y cuatro	700	setecientos
70	setenta	800	ochocientos
75	setenta y cinco	900	novecientos
80	ochenta	1000	mil
86	ochenta y seis		
90	noventa		
97	noventa y seis		

Note that **y** is not used between the hundreds and the tens, but only between the tens and the unit digits.

101	ciento y uno
345	trescientos cuarenta y cinco
465	cuatrocientos sesenta y cinco

Gender agreement occurs with the number 1 and with 200–900. Study the following examples.

231 houses	doscientas treinta y una casas
900 boys	novecientos muchachos
451 women	cuatrocientas cincuenta y una mujeres
31 books	treinta y un libros

Rule. The form **un** is used with masculine nouns. **Una** is used with feminine nouns. For the numbers 200–900, the **-os** ending is used with masculine nouns and **-as** is used with feminine nouns.

Exercise A. Say the following number sequences aloud in Spanish.

1. 1; 11; 100	6. 6; 16; 60; 600
2. 2; 12; 20; 200	7. 7; 17; 70; 700
3. 3; 13; 30; 300	8. 8; 18; 80; 800
4. 4; 14; 40; 400	9. 9; 19; 90; 900
5. 5; 15; 50; 500	10. 52; 67; 75; 86

1,000–2,000,000

1,000	mil
2,000	dos mil
2,500	dos mil quinientos
100,000	cien mil
1,000,000	un millón (de)
2,000,000	dos millones (de)

Note. The preposition **de** is used when a noun follows **millón(es)**.

Ordinal Numbers

1st	primero/a (primer)	6th	sexto/a
2nd	segundo/a	7th	séptimo/a
3rd	tercero/a (tercer)	8th	octavo/a
4th	cuarto/a	9th	noveno/a
5th	quinto/a	10th	décimo/a

Notes.

1. Ordinal numbers agree in gender and number with the nouns they modify.

2. **Primero** and **tercero** drop the final **-o** before a masculine singular noun.

3. Ordinal numbers are generally used only through 10th. Beyond that, cardinal numbers are used.

Exercise B. Select the correct answer.

1. El (tenth) mes del año es octubre. (diez, décimo)
2. Pasan la (third) semana en Italia. (tercer, tercera)
3. Hoy es el (first) de mayo. (uno, primero)
4. Están en la (fifth) fila (row). (cinco, quinta)
5. Felipe (the Second) fue (was) muy famoso. (Dos, Segundo)
6. Leen el (first) capítulo. (primero, primer)
7. Andrés celebra su (eighth) cumpleaños. (ochenta, octavo)

DAYS, MONTHS, SEASONS

The Days of the Week: Los Días de la Semana

lunes	Monday	viernes	Friday
martes	Tuesday	sábado	Saturday
miércoles	Wednesday	domingo	Sunday
jueves	Thursday		

Words Referring to Days:

anteayer	the day before yesterday
ayer	yesterday
hoy	today
mañana	tomorrow
pasado mañana	the day after tomorrow

Notes.

1. The calendar week in Spanish may begin with Monday rather than Sunday (generally in Spain rather than Spanish America).
2. Notice that the days of the week are not capitalized.
3. The articles **el/los** are used to express "on" with a day of the week.

Vamos a la escuela los lunes.	We go to school on Mondays.
Voy a Colorado el viernes.	I'm going to Colorado on Friday.

4. Days of the week that end in -s do not change their form for the plural.

The Months of the Year: Los Meses del Año

enero	January	mayo	May	septiembre	September
febrero	February	junio	June	octubre	October
marzo	March	julio	July	noviembre	November
abril	April	agosto	August	diciembre	December

Note. The months are not capitalized. A date is given in the following way:

Hoy es viernes el tres de marzo	Today is Friday, the third of March.
Mañana es jueves el primero de junio.	Tomorrow is Thursday, the first of June.
¿Sabe Ud. la fecha?	Do you know the date?
Sí, es el ocho de noviembre.	Yes, it is the eighth of November.

The Seasons of the Year: Las Estaciones del Año

la primavera	spring	el otoño	autumn
el verano	summer	el invierno	winter

Exercise C. Express the following in Spanish.

1. Today is Thursday, the tenth of August.

   _____

2. Tomorrow is Wednesday, the fifth of January.

   _____

3. My birthday (cumpleaños) is the third of June.

   _____

4. If (si) today is Monday, tomorrow is Tuesday.

   _____

5. If today is Friday, tomorrow is Saturday.

   _____

Exercise D. Answer in Spanish.

1. ¿Qué día es hoy?

   _____

2. ¿Cuál es la fecha?

   _____

3. ¿Cuándo empieza la primavera?

   _____

4. ¿Cuándo empieza el invierno?

   _____

5. ¿En qué mes empieza el año escolar (school)?

   _____

TELLING TIME: LA HORA

¿Qué hora es?	What time is it?
Es la una.	It's one o'clock.
Son las dos.	It's two o'clock.
Es la una y cuarto.	It's 1:15.
Son las tres y media.	It's 3:30 (or half past three).

Son las diez menos cinco.	It's five to ten.
Son las cuatro menos cuarto.	It's a quarter to four.

Notes.

1. One o'clock is expressed in the singular. From two o'clock on, the time is given in the plural.

2. Time after the hour is expressed with **y** and the minutes, generally up to thirty. A quarter after the hour is expressed by **y cuarto** and half past by **y media**.

3. After half past, time is usually expressed by stating the hour ahead minus (**menos**) the minutes. There is another structure that you will also hear, however.

Faltan cinco para las diez.	It's five to ten. (Literally, "It lacks five for ten.")

4. The 24-hour clock is sometimes used, particularly for departure times at airports or train stations.

5. "At" a certain time is expressed by **a las** and the hour.

Comemos a las dos.	We eat at two.
Ellos salen a las cinco.	They leave at five.

6. Midnight is **medianoche** and noon is **mediodía**. Morning (a.m.) is expressed by **de la mañana** (with a specific time) and in the afternoon or evening (p.m.) is **de la tarde**.

Llegamos a las nueve de la mañana.	We arrive at 9:00 a.m.

Exercise E. Give the following times in Spanish.

1. It's 2:15. _____
2. It's 10:25. _____
3. At 1:10. _____
4. At noon. _____
5. It's 6:00 in the morning (a.m.). _____
6. It's 4:40 in the afternoon. _____
7. At 8:30 in the evening. _____
8. It's 3:45. _____

IRREGULAR PRESENT TENSE VERBS

CLASS 1 STEM-CHANGING VERBS

O > UE

Note. > means "becomes."

Volver

vuelvo	volvemos
vuelves	volvéis
vuelve	vuelven

The following verbs change the stem vowel from "o" to "ue" in all forms except **nosotros** and **vosotros**. Some students find it helpful to think of these as "shoe verbs." The four forms that have the stem change fit into the shoe, and the two that do not are left outside the shoe. The following verbs are Class 1 o>ue verbs.

Common o>ue Verbs

almorzar	to have lunch	oler (o>hue)	to smell
contar	to count, tell	poder	to be able
costar	to cost	probar	to prove, try (food)
devolver	to return (an object)	recordar	to remember
encontrar	to find, meet	sonar	to sound, ring
envolver	to wrap up	soñar	to dream
llover	to rain	volar	to fly
mover	to move	volver	to return
also: jugar (u>ue)	to play		

Ella almuerza en casa.	She has lunch at home.
El libro cuesta diez dólares.	The book costs ten dollars.
¿Recuerdas mi nombre?	Do you remember my name?
Llueve mucho en Seattle.	It rains a lot in Seattle.
Las flores huelen bien.	The flowers smell good.

Notes.

1. The verb **contar** has two meanings, "to count" and "to tell." The first generates the noun **la cuenta** (bill, account) and the second generates **el cuento** (story).

2. When the verb **oler** is conjugated in the present tense, the forms that have a stem-change are preceded by the letter "h."

Oler

huelo	olemos
hueles	oléis
huele	huelen

Exercise A. Fill in the blank with the correct form of the verb indicated in parentheses.

1. ¿_____ tú en la cafetería? (almorzar)
2. Ella _____ el libro a la biblioteca. (devolver)
3. Mis amigos _____ mañana. (volver)
4. Nosotros no _____ ir al cine hoy. (poder)
5. Mi despertador (alarm clock) _____ a las siete. (sonar)
6. Yo no _____ su nombre. (recordar)
7. El avión _____ por el aire. (volar)
8. Vosotros _____ los regalos. (envolver)
9. En la primavera _____ mucho. (llover)
10. Los niños _____ el dinero. (contar)

Exercise B. Answer the following questions. Translate your answer.

1. ¿Cuánto cuesta una docena de huevos?

    _____

2. ¿Dónde almuerza usted generalmente?

    _____

3. ¿Cuándo vuelan los pájaros al sur?

    _____

4. ¿Pueden ustedes trabajar mañana?

    _____

5. ¿Llueve mucho en la ciudad donde usted vive?

    _____

6. ¿Recuerda usted la canción?

    _____

7. ¿A qué hora vuelve usted a casa?

    _____

8. ¿Juega usted al tenis?

    _____

Exercise C. Translate the verb indicated in parentheses into Spanish.

1. Yo no _____ encontrar mis llaves. (can)
2. Las flores _____ bien. (smell)
3. La mujer _____ el paquete. (wraps up)
4. Nosotros siempre _____ el cumpleaños de Rosa. (remember)
5. Tú _____ la tortilla española. (try)
6. El camarero(waiter) _____ la propina. (counts)
7. Vosotros _____ en el parque. (play)
8. Los viernes yo _____ a mi amigo en el restaurante. (meet)

E>IE   **Entender**

entiendo	entendemos
entiendes	entendéis
entiende	entienden

Note. Just as with the o>ue stem-changing verbs, the e>ie verbs do not change in the **nosotros** and **vosotros** forms.

Common e>ie Verbs

calentar	to heat	gobernar	to govern
cerrar	to close	negar	to negate
comenzar	to begin	nevar	to snow
defender	to defend	pensar	to think
despertar	to awaken	perder	to lose
empezar	to begin	quebrar	to break
encender	to light, turn on	querer	to want
entender	to understand	temblar	to tremble

Notes.

1. **Comenzar** and **empezar** both mean "to begin."
2. **Pensar** takes either **en** or **de** depending on the meaning. Study the following examples and rules.

Juan piensa mucho en María.	John thinks a lot about Mary. or: John thinks about Mary a lot.
Juan piensa mucho de María.	John thinks a lot of Mary.
¿En qué piensas?	What are you thinking about?
¿Qué piensas de esta pintura?	What do you think about this painting?
Pienso estudiar más tarde.	I intend to study later.

Rules. When referring to the object of a person's thoughts, use the preposition **en**. To indicate high esteem or when asking for an opinion, use **de**. **Pensar** is combined with another infinitive to refer to intended action.

Exercise D. Fill in the blank with the correct form of the verb indicated in parentheses.

1. En las montañas de Colorado _____ mucho. (nevar)
2. El hombre _____ la ventana. (cerrar)
3. ¿_____ Uds. ir al teatro mañana? (querer)
4. Nosotros no _____ temprano los sábados. (comenzar)
5. El pobre muchacho _____ su brazo. (quebrar)
6. Tú _____ el alemán, ¿no? (entender)
7. Nuestro equipo _____ el primer partido (game). (perder)
8. El ruido (noise) _____ al niño. (despertar)
9. Vosotros siempre _____ a las ocho. (empezar)
10. Ella _____ en la película (film). (pensar)

Exercise E. Translate the verb given in parentheses into Spanish.

1. La señora _____ el agua para preparar el té. (heats up)
2. Los soldados _____ su país. (defend)
3. El bandido _____ cuando entra el policía. (trembles)
4. Estos hombres _____ bien la ciudad. (govern)
5. El año escolar _____ en septiembre. (begins)
6. Nosotros _____ las luces (lights). (turn on)
7. Nunca _____ en Los Angeles. (it snows)
8. Vosotros _____ más postre (dessert). (want)

CLASS 2 STEM-CHANGING VERBS

Second-class verbs have the same changes as first-class verbs in the present tense. They behave somewhat differently in other tenses, however, and that is why they are grouped separately.

e>ie		o>ue	
consentir	to consent	dormir	to sleep
divertirse	to have a good time	morir	to die
herir	to wound		
mentir	to lie		
preferir	to prefer		
sentir	to regret, be sorry		
sugerir	to suggest		

Exercise F. Fill in the blank with the correct form of the verb given in parentheses.

1. Yo _____ ir la fiesta con David. (preferir)

2. ¿No _____ tú ocho horas cada noche? (dormir)

3. El niño no _____ a su mamá. (mentir)

4. ¿Qué color _____ usted? (sugerir)

5. Pocas personas _____ de hambre (hunger) aquí. (morir)

Exercise G. Translate the verb given in parentheses into Spanish.

1. Yo _____ en una cama (bed) grande. (sleep)

2. Julián _____ estudiar en la mañana. (prefers)

3. La profesora _____ el libro por Borges. (suggests)

4. Los testigos (witnesses) no _____ en la corte. (lie)

5. Las flores _____ en el invierno. (die)

CLASS 3 STEM-CHANGING VERBS

Pedir

pido	pedimos
pides	pedís
pide	piden

Note. Third-class stem-changing verbs all end in -ir. In the present tense, the "e" in the stem changes to an "i" in all forms except **nosotros** and **vosotros**.

e>i

corregir	to correct	reír	to laugh
despedir	to fire, dismiss	reñir	to quarrel, scold
elegir	to elect	repetir	to repeat
freír	to fry	seguir	to follow, continue
impedir	to prevent, obstruct	servir	to serve
medir	to measure	sonreír	to smile
pedir	to ask for	vestir	to dress

Notes.

1. The verb **seguir** and any others with that base, such as **conseguir** (to obtain, get) or **perseguir** (to pursue), drop the "u" before an "o," for example, **sigo, consigo, persigo.**

2. The verb **vestir** (to dress) is reflexive when the subject is dressing himself. See Chapter 13 for details.

3. The "g" in **corregir** and **elegir** changes to "j" before "o."

corrijo	I correct
elijo	I elect

Exercise H. Fill in the blank with the correct form of the verb in parentheses.

1. En la mañana Juan _____ dos huevos. (freír)

2. Los estudiantes _____ un representante. (elegir)

3. El jefe (boss) _____ el empleado. (despedir)

4. Nosotros _____ mucho en la clase. (reír)

5. En el restaurante yo _____ enchiladas. (pedir)

6. Vosotros _____ las palabras nuevas. (repetir)

7. Tú _____ a tu hermanita. (vestir)

8. El profesor _____ a sus estudiantes. (corregir)

VERBS ENDING IN -UIR

Incluir (to Include)

incluyo	incluimos
incluyes	incluís
incluye	incluye

Note. Verbs ending in -uir have a "y" in all forms except **nosotros** and **vosotros.**

-uir (-y-)

atribuir	to attribute	distribuir	to distribute
construir	to construct	huir	to flee, escape
contribuir	to contribute	incluir	to include
disminuir	to diminish	sustituir	to substitute

Example.

Rosa contribuye dinero a la iglesia.	Rosa contributes money to the church.

DIÁLOGO

Magda calienta la comida en la cocina de su apartamento. Su amiga Ana María entra.

Magda: Hola, Anamari. ¿Quieres ayudarme?

Ana María: Sí, Magda. Huele muy bien. ¿Qué puedo hacer?

Magda: Puedes poner los platos en la mesa. Juan y Arturo van a llegar en veinte minutos.

Ana María: ¿Qué vamos a comer?

Magda: Una tortilla española. Y después vamos al parque a jugar al tenis.

Ana María: Pero, Magda, creo que llueve.

Magda: ¿Llueve? Qué terrible. ¿Qué piensas que debemos hacer si llueve?

Ana María: Pues, podemos ir al museo.

Magda: No, Anamari, no recuerdas a Arturo. Tenemos que pensar en algo más interesante. ¿Quieres ir al cine?

Ana María: ¿Cuándo comienza?

Magda: En dos horas, más o menos. Voy a mirar por la ventana para ver si llueve.

Un minuto más tarde:

Magda: Sí, Anamari. Es verdad. No podemos jugar al tenis hoy.

VERBS THAT ARE IRREGULAR IN THE FIRST PERSON

-OY VERBS

Dar (to Give)

Person	Singular		Plural	
1st	(yo)	doy	(nosotros, -as)	damos
2nd	(tú)	das	(vosotros, -as)	dáis
3rd	(Ud., él, ella)	da	(Uds., ellos, -as)	dan

Two other verbs follow the same pattern as **dar.**

Person		**Ir (to Go)**	**Estar (to Be)**
1st	(yo)	voy	estoy
2nd	(tú)	vas	estás
3rd	(Ud., él, ella)	va	está
1st	(nosotros, -as)	vamos	estamos
2nd	(vosotros, -as)	váis	estáis
3rd	(Uds., ellos, -as)	van	están

Notes.

1. **Ser,** as you recall from Chapter 7, also has -oy in the first person, for example, "Soy una person práctica."

2. **Ir a** plus an infinitive may be used to refer to the future or to indicate "let's" in the first person plural.

Juan va a estudiar en Londres. John is going to study in London.

Vamos a comer ahora. Let's eat now. (We're going to eat now.)

Exercise A. Translate the following:

1. They are going to the beach.

2. I'm fine today, thanks.

   _____

3. We give the book to Peter.

   _____

4. Let's go to the movies.

   _____

5. When are they going to return?

   _____

6. Do I give the money to the cashier (cajero)?

   _____

7. I'm going to begin tomorrow.

   _____

-G- VERBS

Salir (to Leave, Go Out)

Person	Singular		Plural	
1st	(yo)	salgo	(nosotros, -as)	salimos
2nd	(tú)	sales	(vosotros, -as)	salís
3rd	(Ud., él, ella)	sale	(Uds., ellos, -as)	salen

Six other verbs follow the same pattern as **salir. Oír** has an additional spelling change.

Caer (to Fall)	Hacer (to Do, Make)	Oír (to Hear)	Poner (to Put)	Traer (to Bring)	Valer (to Be Worth)
caigo	hago	oigo	pongo	traigo	valgo
caes	haces	oyes	pones	traes	vales
cae	hace	oye	pone	trae	vale
caemos	hacemos	oímos	ponemos	traemos	valemos
caéis	hacéis	oís	ponéis	traéis	valéis
caen	hacen	oyen	ponen	traen	valen

Notes.

1. The glide consonant "y" appears between the o- and the -e in several forms of **oír.**

2. Three other verbs have a "g" in the first person but differ from the above verbs because of stem changes. However, you may find it convenient to learn them with this group.

Decir (to Say, Tell)	Tener (to Have)	Venir (to Come)
digo	tengo	vengo
dices	tienes	vienes
dice	tiene	viene
decimos	tenemos	venimos

decís	tenéis	venís
dicen	tienen	vienen

Exercise B. Answer in Spanish. Translate your answer.

1. ¿A qué hora vienes a la escuela?

   _____

2. ¿Dónde pone Ud. su tarea?

   _____

3. ¿Hace Ud. todos los ejercicios?

   _____

4. ¿Dices la verdad a tu profesora?

   _____

5. ¿Oye Ud. la música?

   _____

6. ¿Cuándo sales para México?

   _____

7. ¿Qué traes a la clase?

   _____

8. ¿Caes mucho cuando esquias (ski)?

   _____

9. ¿Cuánto vale tu bicicleta?

   _____

10. ¿Tienes una favorita camisa vieja?

   _____

-ZCO VERBS

Conocer (to Be Acquainted)

Person	Singular		Plural	
1st	(yo)	conozco	(nosotros, -as)	conocemos
2nd	(tú)	conoces	(vosotros, -as)	conocéis
3rd	(Ud., él, ella)	conoce	(Uds., ellos, -as)	conocen

Most verbs that end in -cer or -cir have the -zco ending for the first person singular (common exceptions are **hacer** and **decir**).

-zco Verbs

aparecer	to appear	ofrecer	to offer
conocer	to know	parecer	to seem
conducir	to drive, lead	producir	to produce
desaparecer	to disappear	reconocer	to recognize
obedecer	to obey	traducir	to translate

Exercise C. Fill in the blank with the correct form of the verb in parentheses.

1. Yo _____ a todos tus amigos. (recognize)

2. Nosotros _____ las frases al francés. (translate)

3. Tu hermano _____ muy mal. (drives)

4. El sombrero _____ muy caro. (seems)

5. Los estudiantes siempre _____ a la maestra. (obey)

6. Yo _____ cincuenta dólares por la bicicleta. (offer)

7. Ellos no _____ a tu prima. (know)

8. El sol _____ a las siete estos días. (appears)

VER AND SABER

Ver (to See)

Person	Singular		Plural	
1st	(yo)	veo	(nosotros, -as)	vemos
2nd	(tú)	ves	(vosotros, -as)	veis
3rd	(Ud., él, ella)	ve	(Uds., ellos, -as)	ven

Saber (to Know)

Person	Singular		Plural	
1st	(yo)	sé	(nosotros, -as)	sabemos
2nd	(tú)	sabes	(vosotros, -as)	sabís
3rd	(Ud., él, ella)	sabe	(Uds., ellos, -as)	saben

Note. These two verbs are irregular only in the first person. Their precise irregularity is unique.

Exercise D. Translate the following:

1. Do you (tú) see my pencil?

   _____

2. I don't know the date.

   _____

3. We see our friends on Saturdays.

   _____

4. She doesn't know my name.

   _____

5. I see some beautiful trees.

   _____

DIFFERENCES BETWEEN SABER AND CONOCER

Saber is used with information. It also means to know how to do something and is commonly used with an infinitive.

Sabemos tu nombre.	We know your name.
¿Sabe Ud. la hora?	Do you know the time?
Juanito sabe leer.	Johnny knows how to read.

Conocer means "to be acquainted with." It is always used when referring to people or places and may be used to refer to a body of knowledge, such as ancient Greek history, or a language.

Conozco a Angela.	I know Angela.
Ellos conocen el arte italiano.	They're acquainted with Italian art.
Conocemos a Madrid.	We're acquainted with Madrid.

Note. According to the Spanish Royal Academy, **a** is used before the names of cities when they do not have a definite article.

Visitamos a Madrid.

Visitamos La Coruña.

Note the following contrasting uses of **saber** and **conocer:**

¿Sabe Ud. el poema "Romance Sonámbulo" de Federico García Lorca?

No, no sé el poema de memoria, pero lo conozco.

Thus, **saber** implies that the poem is memorized, while **conocer** indicates an acquaintance.

Exercise E. Write the correct form of saber or conocer.

1. Yo _____ que ella no viene a la fiesta.
2. Mi esposo y yo _____ a Nueva York.
3. Mi padre _____ hablar portugués.
4. Ellos _____ al señor Gómez, pero no _____ donde vive.
5. Nosotros no _____ la fecha de hoy.
6. Yo _____ al primo de Juan.
7. ¿_____ Uds. cuántos alumnos hay en la escuela?
8. ¿_____ tú a Cristina?

IDIOMATIC EXPRESSIONS WITH TENER

Tener (to Have)

Person	Singular		Plural	
1st	(yo)	tengo	(nosotros, -as)	tenemos
2nd	(tú)	tienes	(vosotros, -as)	tenéis
3rd	(Ud., él, ella)	tiene	(Uds., ellos, -as)	tienen

1. tener viente años — to be twenty years old
2. tener calor — to be hot
3. tener frío — to be cold
4. tener hambre — to be hungry
5. tener sed — to be thirsty
6. tener miedo — to be afraid
7. tener prisa — to be in a hurry
8. tener razón — to be right
9. tener sueño — to be sleepy

10. ¿Qué tiene Ud.?	What's the matter with you?
11. tener suerte	to be lucky

Note. In all of these expressions, **tener** is followed by a noun. Therefore, "very" is expressed by **mucho/a**, not **muy**.

Tengo mucho sueño.	I'm very sleepy.

Exercise F. Translate the following:

1. Are you hungry?

   _____

2. My friend is fifteen years old.

   _____

3. We're very thirsty.

   _____

4. He is not always right.

   _____

5. She's always in a hurry.

   _____

6. I'm not afraid.

   _____

7. What's the matter with them?

   _____

WEATHER EXPRESSIONS WITH HACER

Hacer (to Do, to Make)

Person	Singular		Plural	
1st	(yo)	hago	(nosotros, -as)	hacemos
2nd	(tú)	haces	(vosotros, -as)	hacéis
3rd	(Ud., él, ella)	hace	(Uds., ellos, -as)	hacen

¿Qué tiempo hace?	How's the weather?
Hace buen tiempo.	The weather's good.
Hace mal tiempo.	The weather's bad.
Hace calor.	It's hot.
Hace fresco.	It's cool.
Hace frío.	It's cold.
Hace sol.	It's sunny.
Hace viento.	It's windy.

Note. In all of these expressions, **hace** is followed by a noun. Therefore, "very" is expressed by **mucho**, not **muy**.

Hace mucho viento.	It's very windy.

Exercise G. Translate the words in parentheses into Spanish.

1. Abrimos la ventana porque (it is hot).

   _____

2. ¿Qué tiempo hace en el invierno? (It is very cold.)

   _____

3. Pasan el día en el campo porque (the weather is good).

   _____

4. A veces (it is windy) en el desierto.

   _____

5. ¿(Is it sunny) en la playa?

   _____

6. (It is not cool) en el sol.

   _____

DISTINGUISHING AMONG TENER, HACER, ESTAR, AND SER

Remember that in certain expressions, all four of the verbs **tener, hacer, estar,** and **ser** may translate as a form of "to be" in English. It is wise to be aware of these expressions, so you don't misuse them. For a while you will need to think consciously about them; later you will know which verb to use because it will simply sound right to you.

Exercise H. Write the correct form of tener, ser, estar, or hacer.

1. Yo _____ mucho sueño.
2. ¿_____ Uds. muy cansados?
3. El tío de Carlos _____ médico.
4. ¿Qué tiempo _____ hoy? _____ mucho calor.
5. Mi abuelo _____ ochenta años.
6. ¿Siempre _____ Ud. razón?
7. El café _____ caliente.
8. El chico _____ calor.
9. Yo _____ en mi clase de español.
10. Mis abuelos _____ españoles.

Exercise I. Translate.

1. We are cold.

   _____

2. He is in a hurry.

   _____

3. They are afraid of cats.

   _____

4. Are you very hungry?

   _____

5. I am lucky.

   _____

6. Who is thirsty?

   _____

PRESENT PROGRESSIVE TENSE

The present progressive is used to indicate an action in progress. The present tense of the auxiliary verb **estar**, **seguir**, **continuar**, **ir**, or **andar** is used with the present participle of the action verb. The most common of these auxiliaries is **estar**. To form a regular present participle, take off the verb's infinitive ending and add the appropriate participle ending. Use this with a form of **estar**.

Estar + Verb	− Infinitive Ending	+ Participle Ending
	-ar	-ando
	-er	-iendo
	-ir	-iendo

Examples.

Estoy hablando mucho.	I'm talking a lot.
Estás mandando una carta.	You are sending a letter.

SOME REGULAR PRESENT PARTICIPLES

bailar	bailando	volver	volviendo
mirar	mirando	abrir	abriendo
comer	comiendo	escribir	escribiendo

Examples.

Estamos bailando el tango.	We are dancing the tango.
Estoy comiendo una manzana.	I'm eating an apple.

PRESENT PARTICIPLES ENDING IN -YENDO

creer	creyendo	oír	oyendo
destruir	destruyendo	traer	trayendo
leer	leyendo		

Rule. If the stem of a verb ends in a vowel, the ending for the present participle is **-yendo**. Whenever an unstressed "i" occurs between two vowels, it changes to a "y."

Examples.

Miguel está trayendo el café.	Mike is bringing the coffee.
Estamos leyendo un poema de Octavio Paz.	We're reading a poem by Octavio Paz.

PRESENT PARTICIPLES OF STEM-CHANGING VERBS

Classes 2 and 3 of the stem-changing verbs that end in **-ir** change the stem vowel from "e" to "i" and from "o" to "u."

decir	diciendo
dormir	durmiendo
morir	muriendo
pedir	pidiendo
repetir	repitiendo
seguir	siguiendo
servir	sirviendo
vestir	vistiendo

Note. The present participle of **poder** is **pudiendo**.

Examples.

Estamos haciendo el trabajo ahora.	We're doing the work now.
Está lloviendo.	It's raining.
El bebito está durmiendo.	The baby is sleeping.
Mi hermano está cantando.	My brother is singing.
¿Qué estás haciendo?	What are you doing?

Exercise A. Write the correct present participle of the verbs given in parentheses.

1. Su amigo está (esperar) el autobús en la esquina. _____
2. Juan y yo estamos (leer) el mismo libro. _____
3. ¿Estáis (dormir) en este momento? _____
4. El camarero está (traer) el postre. _____
5. Siguen (hablar) español. _____
6. Continúa (estudiar) hasta las once. _____
7. ¿Están (vender) los libros? _____
8. Sigo (tocar) la guitarra. _____
9. Mi mamá está (servir) la cena ahora. _____
10. ¿Qué estás (decir)? _____

Exercise B. Rewrite the following sentences using the present progressive.

Model: Aprendemos las palabras.

Estamos aprendiendo las palabras.

1. Viajan por los Estados Unidos.

_____

2. ¿Escribes la carta?

_____

3. El niño corre por la calle.

_____

4. Abrimos las ventanas.

_____

5. Canto en español.

_____

6. ¿Quién explica la lección?

_____

7. Hacen la tarea en casa.

_____

8. ¿Trabajáis en el jardín?

_____

Exercise C. Translate the words in parentheses into Spanish.

Model: Yo (am working) esta mañana.

Yo estoy trabajando esta mañana.

1. Los chicos (are playing) en el campo. _____

2. ¿Quién (is teaching) la lección? _____

3. (It is not raining) en este momento. _____

4. ¿Qué (are you doing) Uds? _____

5. Ellos (are describing) el accidente. _____

6. ¿(Do you continue writing) tú todo el verano? _____

7. Ella (is losing) el partido. _____

8. Yo no (am eating) ahora. _____

PRONOUNS

DIRECT OBJECT PRONOUNS

Subject	Direct Object	Subject	Direct Object
yo	me	nosotros	nos
tú	te	vosotros	os
usted	lo, la	ustedes	los, las
él	lo	ellos	los
ella	la	ellas	las

Notes.

1. A direct object pronoun replaces the noun object that receives the action of the verb.

2. Direct object pronouns stand for things and people.

Juan come la tortilla.	Juan la come.
Juan ve a María.	Juan la ve.

3. Direct object pronouns precede the conjugated verb except in the following two cases. First, if there is an infinitive, the pronoun may either precede the conjugated verb or be attached to the infinitive.

   > Vamos a hacerlo.
   >
   > Lo vamos a hacer.

   Second, if there is a present participle, the pronoun may either precede the conjugated verb or be attached to the participle. When a pronoun is attached to a participle, a written accent is placed over the stressed syllable.

   > Teresa está escribiéndolo.
   >
   > Teresa lo está escribiendo.

4. **No** precedes the object pronoun.

No lo veo.	I don't see it.

5. **Lo** may be used to represent an idea. In many cases, it is not translated into English.

¿No lo sabes?	Don't you know? (it)
Pedro me lo dice.	Pedro tells me.
¿Es guapo Luis? Sí, lo es.	Yes, he is.

6. Some Spanish speakers, particularly in Spain, use the indirect pronouns **le** and **les** as direct objects to refer to people. For example,

Conozco a Juan. Le conozco.

Exercise A. Change the noun to a direct object pronoun.

Model: Los alumnos miran la televisión.

Los alumnos la miran.

1. Comprendemos las palabras. _____
2. Miran a Juan. _____
3. Espero a mi primo. _____
4. Compran los libros. _____
5. ¿Quién vende las blusas? _____

Exercise B. Answer in Spanish using the direct object.

1. ¿Oyen Uds. los aviones? Sí, _____
2. ¿Ven Uds. a los vecinos? No, _____
3. ¿Tienes la revista? Sí, _____
4. ¿Visitas las cuevas (caves)? Sí, _____
5. ¿Aprende Ud. los verbos? Sí, _____

Exercise C. Translate into English.

1. Ellos me conocen. _____
2. ¿Te escuchan? _____
3. Ella os busca. _____
4. El nos espera. _____
5. No puedo oírte. _____

INDIRECT OBJECT PRONOUNS

An indirect object pronoun represents the noun to whom or for whom (or to which or for which) the action is intended.

Subject Form	Indirect Object Form	Subject Form	Indirect Object Form
yo (I)	me (me)	nosotros (we)	nos (us)
tú (you)	te (you)	vosotros (you)	os (you)
Ud., él, ella (you, he, she)	le (you, him, her)	Uds., ellos, ellas (they)	les (you, them)

Juan nos habla.	John talks to us.
Brenda me escribe.	Brenda writes to me.

Exercise D. Change the nouns to pronouns.

Model: Leo a los niños.

Les leo.

1. Juan Martinez da dinero a sus hijos.

_____

2. Paquito no dice la verdad a nosotros.

_____

3. Mando el paquete a mi abuelo.

_____

4. Das una pluma a Javier.

_____

5. Quiero escribir a mis amigos.

Exercise E. Translate into Spanish.

1. He brings me a glass (vaso) of water.

_____

2. She explains the lesson to us.

_____

3. Juan serves us coffee.

_____

4. We tell them the time.

_____

5. Can you (tú) give him the letter?

_____

COMBINING DIRECT AND INDIRECT OBJECT PRONOUNS

Ella me escribe la carta. Me la escribe.

Te doy el libro. Te lo doy.

Le mandamos el paquete a él. Se lo mandamos.

Notes.

1. In some cases, a verb will have both a direct object pronoun and an indirect object pronoun. In such cases, the indirect object precedes the direct object.

2. **Se** replaces **le** and **les** before the other pronouns beginning with l-. **Se** always precedes the other pronouns.

Le mando el cheque a Clara. I send the check to Clare.

Se lo mando. I send it to her.

Les escribimos la nota a ellos. We write the note to them.

Se la escribimos. We write it to them.

Exercise F. Translate.

1. We give the book to Mario.

   _____

   We give it to him.

   _____

2. They send me the invitation.

   _____

   They send it to me.

   _____

3. She brings us the food.

   _____

   She brings it to us.

   _____

4. I teach him the lesson.

   _____

   I teach it to him.

   _____

5. He promises her a trip to Bermuda.

   _____

   He promises it to her.

   _____

PREPOSITIONAL PRONOUNS

para mí	for me	para nosotros	for us
para ti	for you	para vosotros	for you
para él	for him	para ellos	for them
para ella	for her	para ellas	for them
para usted	for you	para ustedes	for you
para sí	for himself, herself, yourself	para sí	for themselves, yourselves

Examples.

La carta es para ti.	The letter is for you.
El regalo es de ellos.	The gift is from them.
Ella va a cenar conmigo.	She's going to have dinner with me.

Notes.

1. When combined with the preposition **con**, the pronouns **mí, ti,** and **sí** become **conmigo, contigo,** and **consigo.**

2. **Mí** and **sí** have accent marks, but **ti** does not.

3. With the exceptions of **mí, ti,** and **sí,** the prepositional pronouns are the same as the subject pronouns.

4. After the words **como** (like), **según** (according to) and **incluso** (including), subject pronouns are used in Spanish. Although these words are regarded as prepositions in English and are followed by object pronouns, they are considered to be relater words in Spanish and are followed by subject pronouns.

RELATIVE PRONOUNS

A relative pronoun introduces a clause that is related to a word in the principal clause (that is, its antecedent). Relative pronouns are not omitted in Spanish as they are in English.

que	that, which, who, whom
quien, quienes	who, whom
el que, la que, los que, las que	the one (ones) who
el cual, la cual, los cuales, las cuales	that, which, who, whom
lo cual, lo que	that which, which
cuyo, cuya, cuyos, cuyas	whose

Notes.

1. The most common relative pronoun is **que**. It refers to both persons and things and may be used as the subject or the object of a verb.

El hombre que trabaja aquí es mi amigo.	The man who works here is my friend.
Conozco a un hombre que trabaja aquí.	I know a man who works here.

2. **Quien** and **quienes** refer to persons only and are generally used after prepositions. **Quien** may be used as a subject to express "he who."

La mujer de quien hablamos es muy simpática.	The woman about whom we are talking is very nice.
Quien come demasiado engorda.	He who eats too much gets fat.

3. **El que** (in all its forms) and **el cual** (in all its forms) are used to clarify a reference, especially if the antecedent is distant or if there are two possible antecedents.

La hermana de Luis, la cual vive en San Juan, es maestra.	Luis's sister, the one who lives in San Juan, is a teacher.

4. **El que** (all forms) and **el cual** (all forms) are used after prepositions of two or more syllables and the prepositions **sin** and **por**.

La puerta por la cual entran es magnífica.	The door through which they enter is magnificent.

5. **Lo que** is always used to express "what" as a relative pronoun.

No entiendo lo que él dice.	I don't understand what he says.
Lo que quiero es la verdad.	What I want is the truth.

6. The relative adjective **cuyo** (in all forms) agrees in number and in gender with the noun it modifies.

Ella es la mujer cuya casa voy a comprar.	She is the woman whose house I'm going to buy.

Exercise G. Select the correct answer.

1. Visito a mi primo, (cuyo, el cual) es pintor.
2. Quiero saber (la cual, lo que) estás pensando.
3. (Lo que, lo cual) dice Tomás es importante.
4. El amor (el cual, que) siente es grande.
5. La mujer con (quien, la cual) Pepe almuerza es bonita.
6. El coche (el que, que) veo es blanco.
7. El artista (cuyos, los cuales) cuadros están aquí, es muy famoso.
8. Pepe me dice (lo cual, lo que) quiere.

DEMONSTRATIVE PRONOUNS

Set 1	Masculine	Feminine	Neuter
this one	éste	ésta	esto
these	éstos	éstas	

Set 2			
that one	ése	ésa	eso
those	ésos	ésas	

Set 3			
that one	aquél	aquéllas	aquello
those	aquéllos	aquéllas	

Notes.

1. Demonstrative pronouns agree in gender and number with the nouns they replace.

2. The first set (1) refers to an object (or objects) close both to the speaker and the person he is speaking to. This set may be used with the adverb **aquí** (here). The second set (2) is distinguished from the third set (3) by distance, either in space, time, or thought. Set 2 refers to something that is removed from the speaker, but that is near the person addressed. Set 3 refers to something that is removed from the speaker and the person addressed.

3. The demonstrative pronouns are distinguished from the demonstrative adjectives by written accent marks. The neuter forms do not need accent marks since there are no neuter adjectives. (See Chapter 21 for a discussion of the demonstrative adjectives.)

4. The pronoun **éste** (all forms) is used to express "the latter" and the pronoun **Aquel** (all forms) may express "the former."

Sara y Rosa son hermanas;
ésta es alta y aquélla es baja.

Sara and Rosa are sisters; the latter is tall and the former is short.

5. The neuter pronouns refer to a whole idea rather than to a specific noun.

No comprendo eso.

I don't understand that.

REFLEXIVE VERBS

Levantarse (to Get Up)

Person	Singular		Plural	
1st	(yo)	me levanto	(nosotros, -as)	nos levantamas
2nd	(tú)	te levantas	(vosotros, -as)	os levantáis
3rd	(Ud., él, ella)	se levanta	(Uds., ellos, -as)	se levantan

Vestirse (to Get Dressed)

Person	Singular		Plural	
1st	(yo)	me visto	(nosotros, -as)	nos vestimos
2nd	(tú)	te vistes	(vosotros, -as)	os vestís
3rd	(Ud., él, ella)	se viste	(Uds., ellos, -as)	se visten

Common Reflexive Verbs

(Letters in parentheses indicate vowel changes that occur in the noninfinitive forms of irregular verbs.)

acostarse (o>ue)	to go to bed	enojarse	to get angry
asustarse	to be frightened	equivocarse	to be mistaken
bañarse	to take a bath	irse	to go away, leave
callarse	to be quiet	lavarse	to wash oneself
cepillarse	to brush oneself	levantarse	to get up
darse cuenta	to realize	llamarse	to be called
desayunarse	to have breakfast	marcharse	to leave
despedirse (e>i)	to say goodbye	pasearse	to take a walk
despertarse (e>ie)	to wake up	peinarse	to comb one's hair

divertirse (e>ie)	to have fun	preocuparse	to worry
dormirse (o>ue)	to fall asleep	quedarse	to stay
enfadarse	to get angry	quitarse	to take off
enterarse (de)	to find out (about)	sentarse (e>ie)	to sit down

Examples.

Conchita se despierta a las siete.	Conchita wakes up at seven.
Me siento en la silla azul.	I sit down in the blue chair.
Nos quedamos en el Hotel Ritz.	We stay at the Ritz Hotel.
¿Os vais mañana?	Are you leaving tomorrow?
¿Te das cuenta de eso?	Do you realize that?

Notes.

1. Strictly speaking, a reflexive verb is one whose subject begins an action that reflects back on itself. The subject and the reflexive object of the verb are the same person.

2. Many reflexive verbs can be used both reflexively and nonreflexively. The reflexive pronoun is used only when the action refers back to the subject.

María acuesta al niño.	Mary puts the child to bed.
María se acuesta.	Mary goes to bed.
Juan baña al perro.	John bathes the dog.
Juan se baña.	John takes a bath.

3. Some reflexive verbs, though they use reflexive pronouns, are really idiomatic rather than reflexive. In some cases, the reflexive intensifies the action of the verb.

Daniel se duerme a las once y duerme ocho horas.	Daniel falls asleep at eleven, and he sleeps eight hours.
El muchacho se lo come.	The boy eats it up.

4. Reflexive pronouns are always attached to affirmative commands but precede negative commands. A written accent is needed over the stressed syllable in the affirmative form.

Lávense las manos.	Wash your hands.
No te preocupes.	Don't worry.

5. If an indirect or direct object is used with a reflexive verb, the reflexive pronoun precedes the indirect or direct object. (Remember it this way: R.I.D. for Reflexive, Indirect, Direct.)

Rita se pone el vestido.	Rita puts on the dress.
Rita se lo pone.	Rita puts it on.

Me compro el traje.	I buy myself the suit.
Me lo compro.	I buy it for myself.

6. Reflexive pronouns generally precede conjugated verbs, but they may be attached to infinitives and present participles. Attachment in these cases is optional.

Me voy a levantar tarde.	I'm going to get up late.
or	
Voy a levantarme tarde.	
Él se está preparando.	He is preparing himself.
or	
Él está preparándose.	

When the reflexive is attached to the participle, a written accent is used to indicate the stress.

7. A reciprocal reflexive may be used to indicate an action two or more agents perform on each other.

Nos escribimos a menudo.	We write each other often.
Ellos se comprenden bien.	They understand each other well.
Vosotros os conocéis, ¿no?	You know each other, don't you?

8. The reflexive pronoun **se** is used to form a passive. See Chapter 28.

Exercise A. Give the correct form of the verb indicated (in the present tense). Translate your answer.

1. Adelita (dormirse) a las diez.   _____
2. ¿Cómo (llamarse) tú?   _____
3. Ellos siempre (despertarse) temprano.   _____
4. Yo (acostarse) tarde los sabados.   _____
5. ¿(Divertirse) Uds.?   _____
6. Mañana nosotros (irse) a España.   _____
7. Hoy Pablo (enterarse) del problema.   _____
8. Tú casi nunca (enfadarse), ¿verdad?   _____
9. Yo (equivocarse). Lo siento.   _____
10. ¿Dónde (quedarse) vosotros?   _____

Exercise B. Translate the words in parentheses.

1. El pobre niño (is frightened).   _____
2. Nosotros (take a walk) por el parque.   _____
3. Ella (leaves) a las cinco.   _____
4. ¿No (have breakfast) vosotros hoy?   _____
5. El señor (takes off) el sombrero.   _____

REGULAR PRETERITE TENSE VERBS

The preterite expresses a simple past action. Here are some examples in English in the affirmative, negative, and interrogative.

Affirmative	Negative	Interrogative
I sang last night.	I didn't sing. . . .	Did I sing . . . ?
They went to the store.	They didn't go. . . .	Did they go . . . ?
He learned how to do it.	He didn't learn . . .	Did he learn . . . ?

Common Indicators of Past Time

yesterday	ayer
last night	anoche
last Saturday	el sábado pasado
last week	la semana pasada
ago	hace
a month ago	hace un mes
two years ago	hace dos años

-AR VERBS The preterite is formed by removing the -ar from the infinitive and adding the following endings: -é, -aste, -ó, -amos, -asteis, -aron.

Cantar

Person	Singular		Plural	
1st	(yo)	canté	(nosotros, as)	cantamos
2nd	(tú)	cantaste	(vosotros, -as)	cantasteis
3rd	(Ud., él, ella)	cantó	(Uds., ellos, -as)	cantaron

Notes.

1. Class 1 verbs have no stem change in the preterite. For example,

    Pepe encuentra la llave en el cajón (drawer).

    Pepe encontró la llave en el cajón.

2. Verbs ending in -car,-gar and -zar have a spelling change in the first person form of the preterite. In order to maintain the [k] sound, the "c" is replaced by "qu." In order to maintain the [g] sound, a "u" is inserted before the ending. The "z" in -zar verbs changes to a "c."

Examples.

buscar	yo busqué
marcar	yo marqué
pagar	yo pagué
llegar	yo llegué
almorzar	yo almorcé
comenzar	yo comencé

Exercise A. Fill in the blank with the correct form of the verb indicated in the preterite tense. Translate your answer.

Model: Anoche yo _____ la rumba. (bailar)

Anoche yo bailé la rumba.

Last night I danced the rumba.

1. Ellos _____ mucho dinero por el coche. (pagar)

   _____

2. Diego _____ el paquete al correo (post office). (llevar)

   _____

3. Mi tío _____ en Saudi Arabia el año pasado. (trabajar)

   _____

4. ¿No _____ tú el disco de Jimi Hendrix? (escuchar)

   _____

5. Ayer nosotros _____ los libros en casa. (dejar)

   _____

6. Vosotros no _____ hasta (until) esta mañana,¿no? (regresar)

   _____

7. ¿_____ los Padres el partido de béisbol el sábado pasado?
   (ganar) _____

8. La semana pasada Anita _____ unos zapatos muy elegantes.
   (comprar) _____

9. Nosotros _____ las pinturas de Picasso en el museo. (mirar)

   _____

10. ¿No _____ tú a Emilia a comer con nosotros? (invitar)

    _____

11. Ayer yo _____ en Jack in the Box. (almorzar)

    _____

12. Yo _____ la teoría a mi hermano. (explicar)

_____

Exercise B. Change the verb from the present to the preterite.

Model: Ella prepara una comida deliciosa.

Ella preparó una comida deliciosa.

1. Tú bailas muy bien, Carmen. _____

2. El tren llega a las once. _____

3. ¿Qué pasa, Enrique? _____

4. ¿Regresan ellos a las cinco? _____

5. Ganamos un televisor en el sorteo (drawing). _____

6. Los niños cuentan de uno a diez. _____

7. Vosotros habláis muy bien el español. _____

8. Necesitamos ir al mercado. _____

9. ¿Por qué compras zapatos verdes? _____

10. Pregunto la hora. _____

Exercise C. Translate the following sentences.

1. They met Jaime in the library.

_____

2. Did you (tú) try (probar) the guacamole? It's delicious!

_____

3. I traveled through (por) México last summer.

_____

4. He remembered the words and finished (terminar) the translation (traducción).

_____

5. What did you dream last night?

_____

6. Mariana studied Spanish three years ago.

_____

7. We ate lunch at Brian's house last Sunday.

_____

8. Did you (tú) help Melissa with her homework?

_____

9. Where did they spend the weekend (fin de semana)?

_____

10. We had coffee with her, and we talked about Argentina.

_____

-ER AND
-IR VERBS
The preterite of the -er and -ir verbs are formed by dropping the infinitive ending and adding -í, -iste, -ió, -imos, isteis, ieron.

Comer

Person	Singular		Plural	
1st	(yo)	comí	(nosotros, -as)	comimos
2nd	(tú)	comiste	(vosotros, -as)	comisteis
3rd	(Ud., él, ella)	comió	(Uds., ellos, -as)	comieron

Vivir

Person	Singular		Plural	
1st	(yo)	vivi	(nosotros, -as)	vivimos
2nd	(tú)	viviste	(vosotros, -as)	vivisteis
3rd	(Ud., él, ella)	vivió	(Uds., ellos, -as)	vivieron

Notes.

1. Class 1 stem-changing verbs are regular in the preterite.

2. The preterite form **vio** from **ver** (to see) does not have a written accent mark.

Exercise D. Change the verb form to agree with the new subject.

Model: Manolo abrió la ventana.   Tú _____

Tú abriste la ventana.

1. Ellos corrieron cinco millas.   Yo _____
2. ¿Dónde escondiste mis llaves?   Ud. _____
3. Gabriel no comprendió muy bien.   Nosotros_____
4. Ella prometió estar aquí temprano.   Ellos _____
5. Conchita rompió su plato favorito.   Tú _____
6. Metí el dinero en la cartera (wallet).   Él_____
7. Comimos en casa ayer.   Mi abuelo _____
8. Juanito perdió su pluma.   Yo _____
9. Encendí la luz en la cocina.   Tú _____
10. Ellos entendieron bien la lección.   Nosotros_____

Exercise E. Answer the following questions in Spanish. Translate your answer.

Model: ¿Perdiste las llaves?

No, no perdí las llaves.

No, I didn't lose the keys.

1. ¿Comprendieron Uds. la pregunta?

_____

_____

2. ¿Corrió Ud. por el parque ayer?

_____

_____

3. ¿Dónde asistió Ud. (attend) a la escuela?

_____

_____

4. ¿Prometiste ir al cine con José?

_____

_____

5. ¿Rompió Ud. el disco?

_____

_____

6. ¿Viviste en Chile el año pasado?

_____

_____

7. ¿Comiste mucho durante las vacaciones de Navidad (Christmas)?

_____

_____

8. ¿Recibiste un regalo de tu tía favorita?

_____

_____

9. ¿Escribieron Uds. a sus abuelos?

_____

_____

10. ¿Subieron ellos la montaña?

_____

_____

11. ¿Sufriste mucho cuando aprendiste los verbos?

_____

_____

DIÁLOGO   Una Visita

Ayer Josefina visitó a su amiga Clara. Cuando ella llegó allí, Clara abrió la puerta. Las dos mujeres pasaron a la sala donde tomaron café y galletas y hablaron.

Josefina: Esta mañana recibí una tarjeta postal de Beatriz.

Clara: Maravilloso. ¿Y qué dice? ¿Todavía está en Francia?

Josefina: No, en Grecia. Salió de Francia la semana pasada. Dice que vio los museos en París, comió bien en los restaurantes allí, y compró muchas cosas.

Clara: ¿Cuándo va a regresar?

Josefina: En dos semanas. Hablé con su hermano antes de venir aquí y vamos a organizar una fiesta para Beatriz. ¿Quieres ayudarnos?

Clara: Sí, buena idea.

Exercise F. Preguntas sobre el diálogo.

1. ¿A quién visitó Josefina?
2. ¿Dónde tomaron café y galletas?
3. ¿Dónde está Beatriz ahora?
4. ¿Qué escribió Beatriz de Francia?
5. ¿Cuándo regresa Beatriz?

IRREGULAR PRETERITE TENSE VERBS

IR, SER, DAR

Ir/Ser

Person	Singular		Plural	
1st	(yo)	fui	(nosotros, -as)	fuimos
2nd	(tú)	fuiste	(vosotros, -as)	fuisteis
3rd	(Ud., él, ella)	fue	(Uds., ellos, -as)	fueron

Dar

Person	Singular		Plural	
1st	(yo)	di	(nosotros, -as)	dimos
2nd	(tú)	diste	(vosotros, -as)	disteis
3rd	(Ud., él, ella)	dio	(Uds., ellos, -as)	dieron

Notes.

1. **Ir** and **ser** have the same forms in the preterite.
2. **Dar** follows the -er/-ir pattern.

Exercise A. Change from the present to the preterite.

1. Soy profesor.

_____

2. Ellos van a la playa.

_____

3. Nuestro vecino (neighbor) es médico.

_____

4. Nosotros damos una fiesta grande.

_____

5. Arturo va con su novia.

_____

6. Yo no doy nada.

_____

Exercise B. Answer in Spanish.

1. ¿Fuiste al cine anoche?

_____

2. ¿Quién fue el primer presidente?

_____

3. ¿Fueron Uds. al concierto?

_____

4. ¿Dio Ud. una conferencia (lecture)?

_____

5. ¿Dieron Uds. el dinero a sus padres?

_____

OTHER STEM-CHANGING VERBS

-UVE- Stem-Changing Verbs

Andar (to Walk)		Estar		Tener	
anduve	anduvimos	estuve	estuvimos	tuve	tuvimos
anduviste	anduvisteis	estuviste	estuvisteis	tuviste	tuvisteis
anduvo	anduvieron	estuvo	estuvieron	tuvo	tuvieron

Note. Verbs that consist of a prefix plus **tener** follow the same pattern as **tener**. Examples are **obtener, mantener, sostener**.

-U- Stem-Changing Verbs

Saber		Poder		Poner	
supe	supimos	pude	pudimos	puse	pusimos
supiste	supisteis	pudiste	pudisteis	pusiste	pusisteis
supo	supieron	pudo	pudieron	puso	pusieron

Note. The irregular verb **caber** (to fit) follows this pattern:

cupe, cupiste, cupo, cupimos, cupisteis, cupieron

Examples.

No pude hacerlo.	I wasn't able to do it.
Todos no cupieron en el coche.	They didn't all fit in the car.
Ella puso la comida en la mesa.	She put the food on the table.

Hacer, Querer, Venir

Hacer		Querer		Venir	
hice	hicimos	quise	quisimos	vine	vinimos
hiciste	hicisteis	quisiste	quisisteis	viniste	vinisteis
hizo	hicieron	quiso	quisieron	vino	vinieron

Note. The letter "c" changes to a "z" before an -o in the conjugation of **hacer** in order to preserve the pronunciation: either the SESEO [s] or the CECEO [θ].

Verbs with -J-

Decir	
dije	dijimos
dijiste	dijisteis
dijo	dijeron

Traer	
traje	trajimos
trajiste	trajisteis
trajo	trajeron

Traducir	
traduje	tradujimos
tradujiste	tradujisteis
tradujo	tradujeron

Notes.

1. Notice that the form for **Uds./ellos/ellas** ends in -jeron.
2. Other verbs that end in -ucir follow the same pattern as **traducir** (for example, **producir, conducir**).

Exercise C. Give the preterite tense of the verb in parentheses.

1. ¿Qué (traer) Ud. para beber? _____
2. Yo (saber) la verdad. _____
3. ¿Dónde (poner) tú los libros? _____
4. Juan y yo (tener) que estudiar ayer. _____
5. Ellos (estar) en la biblioteca por una hora. _____
6. Tú no (poder) encontrar el dinero. _____
7. Ellos (decir) la historia. _____
8. Él (andar) por la playa. _____
9. Los papeles no (caber) en el cuaderno. _____
10. ¿Qué (hacer) tú el sábado? _____

Exercise D. Change the verbs from the present to the preterite.

1. Ella no puede ir. _____
2. Mi padre conduce el otro coche. _____
3. La chica no dice nada. _____
4. Yo no traduzco todas las frases. _____
5. Nosotros venimos a tiempo. _____
6. Estáis aquí temprano. _____
7. Detiene el autobús. _____
8. ¿Qué hace ella? _____
9. Traigo un regalo para ti. _____
10. ¿Dónde ponemos los platos? _____

Exercise E. Answer in Spanish.

1. ¿Vinieron Uds. a la escuela el sábado?

_____

2. ¿Dónde estuvo Ud. anoche?

   _____

3. ¿Tradujiste el párrafo?

   _____

4. ¿Condujeron Uds. a La Paz el año pasado?

   _____

5. ¿Tuviste que escribir una composición ayer?

   _____

Exercise F. Translate the English words into Spanish.

1. Nosotros (did not bring) suficiente dinero.   _____
2. Yo (was able) entender la lección.   _____
3. Concha (did) toda la tarea.   _____
4. ¿Qué (did he say) en la reunión?   _____
5. Todos no (fit) en el coche.   _____
6. Mi abuelo (came) para celebrar mi cumpleaños.   _____
7. Nosotros (were) en el Brasil el año pasado.   _____
8. Ayer yo (put) el papel en el escritorio (desk).   _____

VERBS IN WHICH "Y" REPLACES "I"

Creer		Leer		Oír	
creí	creímos	leí	leímos	oí	oímos
creiste	creisteis	leiste	leisteis	oiste	oisteis
creyó	creyeron	leyó	leyeron	oyó	oyeron

Notes.

1. Notice that the expected ending -ió becomes -yó and -ieron becomes -yeron when the verb stem ends in a vowel.

2. Verbs that end in -uir follow this pattern.

Exercise G. Change the verb to the preterite.

1. Leen una novela.   _____
2. Oigo las campanas (bells).   _____
3. La tormenta (storm) destruye las plantas.   _____
4. ¿Quién cree el cuento?   _____
5. Los niños caen en la nieve.   _____

Exercise H. Answer in Spanish.

1. ¿Oyeron Uds. los aviones?

   _____

2. ¿Leyó Ud. el artículo?

   _____

3. ¿Caiste de la cama anoche?

_____

4. ¿Creyeron Uds. a Juan?

_____

5. ¿Contribuyó Ud. parte de su sueldo (salary)?

_____

CLASS 2 STEM-CHANGING VERBS

Preferir	
preferí	preferimos
preferiste	preferisteis
prefirió	prefirieron

Dormir	
dormí	dormimos
dormiste	dormisteis
durmió	durmieron

Note. Class 2 stem-changing verbs have a stem change in the third person singular and plural: "i" for verbs such as **preferir** (**mentir, sentir,** and **sugerir**), and "u" for **dormir** and **morir.**

Exercise I. Translate the verb indicated into Spanish.

1. El testigo (witness) (didn't lie) en la corte. _____
2. El camarero (suggested) la especialidad del día. _____
3. Mis padres (slept) bien anoche. _____
4. El empleado del hotel (regretted) el error en la cuenta. _____
5. Nosotros (preferred) ver la otra película. _____
6. El pobre perro (died) de hambre. _____

CLASS 3 STEM-CHANGING VERBS

Seguir	
seguí	seguimos
seguiste	seguiste
siguió	siguieron

Notes.

1. The third person singular and plural of Class 3 stem-changing verbs have an "i" in the stem.

2. Note that verbs ending in -guir (**seguir, conseguir, perseguir**) have a "u" following the "g" to preserve the sound [g].

3. Common third-class verbs are as follows: **despedir, freír, impedir, medir, pedir, reír, reñir, repetir, servir, sonreír** and **corregir.**

Exercise J. Write the correct form of the verb in the preterite.

1. Yo (corregir) el examen. _____
2. Ramón (pedir) una Coca Cola. _____
3. ¿Quién (servir) la comida? _____

4. Carlota (medir) el cuarto antes de comprar muebles. _____

5. El cocinero (freír) los huevos. _____

6. Tú (repetir) las palabras correctamente. _____

7. El niño (sonreír) cuando vio a su padre. _____

8. ¿Cuándo (despedir) ellos de Pepe? _____

Exercise K. Change to the preterite.

1. Sigues el mismo camino. _____

2. Siempre riño con mi hermana. _____

3. Gloria y Marco sonríen mucho. _____

4. La señora Lozano corrige la composición. _____

5. ¿A qué hora sirves la comida? _____

REVIEW EXERCISE

Exercise L. Translate the English words into Spanish.

1. Yo (walked) a la escuela. _____

2. ¿Quién (brought) las cintas (tapes)? _____

3. ¿(Did you read) Uds. el periódico hoy? _____

4. Su amigo (did not say) una palabra. _____

5. Nosotros (went) a casa temprano ayer. _____

6. Yo (drove) el coche de mi amigo. _____

7. Sofía (repetir) la frase en voz alta (aloud). _____

8. Ellos no (dar) el cheque a Miguel. _____

9. ¿(Did you go) tú al partido (game) ayer? _____

10. La profesora no (believed) al niño. _____

Chapter 16

IMPERFECT TENSE

The imperfect expresses a past action that is seen as continuing or habitual. Neither the end nor the beginning is expressed. The focus is on the pictorial past, an action in progress. In the next chapter you will see just how the imperfect and the preterite differ and how to use both in describing past activities. For now, let's see some examples of the imperfect. Notice the various possibilities in English.

¿Qué hacían Uds?	What were you doing?
Bailábamos y cantábamos.	We were dancing and singing.
De vez en cuando íbamos al teatro.	From time to time, we would go to the theater.
Comíamos allí a menudo.	We used to eat there often.

-AR VERBS   All -ar verbs are regular in the imperfect. The imperfect is formed by removing the infinitive ending and adding the following endings: -aba, -abas, -aba, -ábamos, -abais, -aban.

Hablar

Person	Singular		Plural	
1st	(yo)	hablaba	(nosotros, -as)	hablábamos
2nd	(tú)	hablabas	(vosotros, -as)	hablabais
3rd	(Ud., él, ella)	hablaba	(Uds., ellos, -as)	hablaban

Note. The **nosotros** form has a written accent mark: **hablábamos.**

Exercise A. Change the following present tense verbs to the imperfect.

Model: Juan camina todos los días.

Juan caminaba todos los días.

1. Trabajamos cada (each) viernes.

_____

2. Ellos cenan a las ocho los domingos.

_____

3. Doy de comer (feed) a mi perro dos veces al día.

_____

4. Ella gasta (spends) demasiado en la tienda de ropa.

_____

5. Siempre estáis ocupados los sábados.

_____

6. Durante el verano, nadamos (swim) en el lago.

_____

7. A veces Paco y Marta almuerzan en un café francés.

_____

8. Busco un anuncio en el periódico.

_____

9. El rey (king) viaja a Grecia en agosto.

_____

10. Pienso escribir un poema.

_____

-ER, -IR VERBS

To form the imperfect of -er and -ir verbs, take off the ending of the infinitive and add the following endings: -ía, -ías, -ía, -íamos, -íais, -ían.

Comer

Person	Singular		Plural	
1st	(yo)	comía	(nosotros, -as)	comíamos
2nd	(tú)	comías	(vosotros, -as)	comíais
3rd	(Ud., él, ella)	comía	(Uds., ellos, -as)	comían

Note. There are only three irregular verbs in the -er/-ir category. They are presented after the exercise on the regular verbs.

Exercise B. Change the verbs from the present to the imperfect.

1. Quiero ir a Puerto Vallarta durante las vacaciones. _____

2. Jorge no devuelve los libros a la biblioteca a tiempo. _____

3. Ellos no pueden venir el diez de marzo. _____

4. No sé su nombre. _____

5. Siempre hacemos muchas preguntas. _____

6. Al entrar a la clase, el profesor dice, — Buenos días, jóvenes. _____

7. La familia Martínez contribuye mucho dinero a la iglesia. _____

8. ¿No oyes la música? _____

9. Cada mañana salgo a las siete y media. _____

10. Mi mamá siempre pide café con leche. _____

VERBS THAT ARE IRREGULAR IN THE IMPERFECT

Ser	
era	éramos
eras	erais
era	eran

Ir	
iba	íbamos
ibas	ibais
iba	iban

Ver	
veía	veíamos
veías	veíais
veía	veían

Exercise C. Change the verbs from the present to the imperfect.

1. El señor López es gerente (manager) de un restaurante. _____

2. Cada mes vamos a visitar a Julia. _____

3. A veces vemos al Doctor Beltrán en la clínica. _____

4. Cuando voy a París, visito los museos. _____

5. Tú eres un estudiante magnífico. _____

REVIEW EXERCISE

Exercise D. Fill in the blank with the correct form of the verb in the imperfect.

1. Los estudiantes _____ que leer un libro cada mes. (tener)

2. Yo no _____ todas las repuestas (answers). (saber)

3. Nosotros no _____ cartas todos los días. (recibir)

4. Durante las vacaciones, ellos _____ tarde a menudo. (acostarse)

5. Mi hermana siempre _____ mucho ropa de moda (fashionable). (comprar)

6. Las niñas _____ en el patio frecuentemente. (jugar)

7. La abuela _____ comidas deliciosas cada domingo. (preparar)

8. Nosotros _____ al parque mucho el año pasado. (ir)

9. Ella _____ frecuentemente a su novio. (ver)

10. Ellos _____ buenos amigos. (ser)

A COMPARISON OF PRETERITE AND IMPERFECT

THE DIFFERENCE BETWEEN PRETERITE AND IMPERFECT

The preterite expresses a completed past action, generally focusing on the beginning or the end of the action. The imperfect expresses a continuing past action. If we visualize the past as a play, the description of the stage would be given in the imperfect.

Hacía frío cuando fuimos al parque.	It was cold when we went to the park.
Ellos bailaban y cantaban.	They were singing and dancing.
¿Qué hacías cuando te llamé?	What were you doing when I called you?
Sabías que llegaron ayer?	Did you know they arrived yesterday?

Note. Several verbs have a slight change in meaning when changed from imperfect to preterite:

saber	Juan sabía eso.	John knew that.
	Juan supo eso.	John found that out.
conocer	Marta conocía a Paco.	Martha used to know Paco.
	Marta conoció a Paco.	Martha met Paco.
poder	No podíamos ir.	We weren't able to go.
	Pudimos ir.	We managed to go.

Exercise A. Choose the preterite or the imperfect.

1. (Eran, fueron) las ocho cuando Juan llegó. _____

2. (Salió, salía) en seguida (right away). _____

3. (Comimos, comíamos) en el restaurante anoche. _____

4. Los estudiantes alemanes (volvieron, volvían) a su país el año pasado. _____

5. Margarita y yo (recibimos, recibíamos) muchos
regalos para la Navidad.   _____

6. ¿(Visitaste, Visitabas) el museo ayer?   _____

7. (Hablé, Hablaba) con María cuando   _____
su mamá (entró, entraba).   _____

8. Siempre (me levantaba, me levanté) a las siete. _____

9. Durante las vacaciones yo (vi, veía) a Carlos
con frecuencia.   _____

10. ¿(Fue, Iba) Ud. a la tienda anoche?   _____

11. La casa (fue, era) muy grande.   _____

12. Roberto (tenía, tuvo) una bicicleta pero   _____
la (vendió, vendía).   _____

**Exercise B. Fill in the blank with the correct form of the verb in parentheses
(preterite or imperfect).**

1. Yo (left) de casa a las seis.   _____

2. Cuando yo (was) joven, vivía en México.   _____

3. Ellos (were) altos y   _____
(had) ojos azules.   _____

4. El siempre (would go) al cine los sábados.   _____

5. ¿Qué (were you doing) tú a las doce?   _____

6. (There were) mucha gente en la playa.   _____

7. Rodrigo (put on) el sueter   _____
porque él (was) frío.   _____

8. Mi madre (was) veiente y ocho años   _____
cuando yo (was born) (nacer).   _____

9. Yo (met) a Marta en una fiesta.   _____

10. (Did he dance) con Raquel?   _____

LECTURA   Cuando Andrés era joven, vivía en Madrid cerca del Retiro, un parque muy
bonito. Iba al Retiro con su familia o con sus amigos los domingos. Había un
lago allí donde podían alquilar barcos. A veces, después de pasar dos horas
en el parque, iban a un restaurante a comer. En Madrid siempre había
muchas actividades interesantes: el teatro, las corridas de toros, los museos,
los partidos de fútbol, la Casa de Campo, los cines, y muchas otras cosas.
Andrés pensaba que Madrid era la mejor ciudad del mundo.

Cuando Andrés tenía dieciséis años, fue a visitar a un primo que tenía en
Barcelona. Su primo, Rodrigo, vivía cerca del Parque Güell, un parque
diseñado por el arquitecto Antonio Gaudí. Desde allí había una vista
magnífica del Mar Mediterraneo, y Andrés vio el Mediterraneo por la
primera vez. Tenía muchas ganas de ir a la playa. En Barcelona no hay
buenas playas, pero cerca de allí hay unos resortes magníficos.

Andrés fue con sus tíos y Rodrigo a Tossa de Mar, una pequeña ciudad al
norte de Barcelona en la Costa Brava. Se quedaron en el Hotel Ancora,
donde podían ver la playa de Tossa desde el balcón. El clima era perfecto, el

agua era un azul brillante, y las montañanas alrededor de Tossa eran bellísimas. Andrés pensaba que estaba en el paraíso, y se dijo — Algún día quiero vivir en la Costa Brava.

El único problema que Andrés tenía en esa parte de España era la lengua: el Catalán. Las personas de Cataluña no hablan español como lengua primera. Hablan Catalán. Pero aprenden el español más tarde. Muchos catalanes van a las escuelas bilingües donde estudian en catalán y en español. Andrés tenía muchas dificultades con el catalán y hablaba español con sus parientes.

Cuando Andrés volvió a Madrid se dio cuenta de que las dos ciudades más grandes de España, Madrid y Barcelona, son muy diferentes. Tienen diferentes lenguas, historias, y climas. Andrés se alegraba de saber más de su país. Y también, tenía una nueva ciudad favorita: Tossa de Mar.

Exercise C. Preguntas sobre la lectura.

1. ¿Dónde vivía Andrés?

   _____

2. ¿Qué es el Retiro?

   _____

3. ¿Qué hacía Andrés los domingos?

   _____

4. ¿Adónde fue Andrés?

   _____

5. ¿Dónde vivían sus parientes?

   _____

6. ¿Cómo se llama la ciudad en la Costa Brava que visitaron?

   _____

7. ¿Qué es el catalán?

   _____

EXPRESSIONS OF TIME: HACER WITH PRESENT, IMPERFECT, AND PRETERITE

USING HACE WITH THE PRESENT TENSE

In order to express an action which began in the past and is continuing in the present, Spanish uses the following construction:

hace + period of time + que + verb in present tense

Hace dos días que estoy aquí. (Literally: It makes two days that I am here.)	I've been here for two days.
Hace tres años que vivimos en California.	We've lived in California for three years.
¿Cuánto tiempo hace que sabes manejar?	How long have you known how to drive?

Exercise A. Choose the correct translation for the words in parentheses from the column on the right.

1. Hace dos horas que ellos (have waited)   a. estudia   _____

2. ¿Cuánto tiempo hace que Patricia (has studied) español?   b. esperan   _____

3. Hace tres años que David (has worked).   c. estamos   _____

4. Hace un mes que (we've been) aquí.   d. estás   _____

5. ¿Cuánto tiempo hace que (tú) (have been) aquí?   e. trabaja   _____

USING HACÍA WITH THE IMPERFECT

Hacía is used with the imperfect to express an action that began and ended in the past. Study the following examples.

Hacía dos semanas que estabámos allí.	We had been there for two weeks.

Hacía una hora que jugábamos.	We had been playing for an hour.
¿Cuánto tiempo hacía que trabajabas?	How long had you been working?

Exercise B. Translate into Spanish.

1. They had been listening to the record for an hour.

   _____

2. How long had they been here?

   _____

3. He had been sick for two days.

   _____

4. We had been talking for an hour.

   _____

5. Elsa had been reading for 15 minutes.

   _____

USING HACE WITH THE PRETERITE

To express "ago," Spanish uses **hace** plus a period of time and the preterite tense. While the expression of time generally follows the verb, it may also precede the verb. If so, **que** separates the two units.

Juan llegó hace una hora. (Literally: John arrived it makes an hour.)	John arrived an hour ago.
¿Cuánto tiempo hace que empezaste?	How long ago did you begin?
Hace media hora que Julia se despertó.	Julia woke up half an hour ago.

Exercise C. Translate into Spanish.

1. They came two hours ago.

   _____

2. How long ago did you (tú) eat?

   _____

3. I visited New York two years ago.

   _____

4. We saw Mr. Robles three days ago.

   _____

5. How long ago did she work there?

   _____

REVIEW EXERCISE

Exercise D. Translate into Spanish.

1. We went to Spain two years ago.

   _____

2. My sister has been sleeping for an hour.

   _____

3. They had been running for thirty minutes.

   _____

4. How long have you (tú) been reading?

   _____

5. It's been raining for a long time.

   _____

6. How long had they been there?

   _____

GUSTAR AND SIMILAR VERBS

GUSTAR Gustar means "to please," an idea commonly expressed in English as "to like." When **gustar** is translated as "to like," the subject and the object are the reverse of what they are in the English expression.

Examples.

Me gusta mucho tu casa.	Your house pleases me a lot. (I like your house a lot.)
Esto te va a gustar mucho.	You're going to like this a lot.
Nos gusta viajar.	We like to travel.
A Raul le gustan los deportes.	Raul likes sports.

Notes.

1. **Gustar** is used with the indirect object pronouns. If clarification is needed, the preposition **a** is used with the appropriate prepositional pronoun, for example, "A ellos les gusta la novela." The prepositional pronouns may also be added for emphasis, for example, "A mí no me gustan las albóndigas (meatballs)."

2. While the most common forms of **gustar** are **gusta** and **gustan,** it is also possible to say "Me gustas" (I like you, or literally, you please me) and "Te gusto." (You like me, or literally, I please you).

3. When an infinitive is used as the subject of **gustar,** it functions as a singular noun, and **gusta** is the form of the verb.

Exercise A. Write the correct form of gustar in the present.

1. No me _____ el lunes.
2. No les _____ la tarea.
3. Me _____ mucho escribir composiciones.
4. Nos _____ cenar en el restaurante chino.
5. Al joven le _____ todos los animales.
6. ¿No te _____ las ciudades grandes?

Exercise B. Translate into Spanish using the indicated tense: present, preterite, or imperfect.

1. (We liked) la música.   _____

2. (They like) el invierno porque esquían. _____

3. (Do you (tú) like) las corridas de toros? _____

4. (I didn't like) la contaminación del aire. _____

5. ¿(Didn't he like) sus vecinos (neighbors)? _____

6. Cuando ellos vivían allí, (they liked) ir a las montañas durante los fines de semana. _____

Exercise C. Add "a" and the appropriate prepositional pronoun for clarification or emphasis of the object given in English.

1. (Him) no le gusta la música de Ozzie Osborne. _____

2. (Us) nos gustan mucho las pinturas de Chagall. _____

3. ¿(You fam. sing.) no te gusta el clima aquí? _____

4. No me gusta (me) tampoco. _____

5. (Her) le gustaría estudiar en Francia. _____

SOME VERBS THAT FUNCTION IN THE SAME MANNER AS GUSTAR

doler	to ache	faltar	to lack, to be missing
encantar	to delight (to love an activity or thing)	hacer falta	to need
		quedar	to have left

Me duele la cabeza.

My head aches. (I have a headache.)

¿No te encanta la Costa Brava?

Don't you love the Costa Brava?

Te falta un botón.

You're missing a button.

Me hace falta practicar el español.

I need to practice Spanish.

¿Cuánta comida nos queda?

How much food do we have left (over)?

Note. For these verbs, the subject is the equivalent of the English direct object, and the indirect object is the same as the English subject. Other Spanish verbs that follow the same pattern in Spanish but that translate literally into English are **pasar** (to happen), **enojar** (to anger), **interesar** (to interest), **parecer** (to seem) and **sorprender** (to surprise). The object pronoun is used with these verbs even when the noun appears.

Examples.

Me interesa mucho la historia.

History interests me a lot.

Nos parece una buena idea.

It seems like a good idea to us.

¿Te sorprende eso?

Does that surprise you?

Exercise D. Translate into Spanish.

1. (I need) trabajar mañana. _____

2. (We love) la música cubana. _____

3. (You (tú) don't have left) bastante azúcar. _____

4. (It seems to her) una buena idea. _____

5. Las leyendas mexicanas (interest us) mucho. _____

6. Su visita (surprised us). _____

7. ¿Qué les (happened to them)? _____

NEGATIVE AND AFFIRMATIVE WORDS

Negative	Affirmative
nada (nothing)	algo/todo (something/everthing)
nadie (no one)	alguien/todo el mundo (someone/everyone)
nunca/jamás (never/not ever)	siempre/a veces/ algunas veces (always/sometimes)
ningún (none, not any, no)	algún (some)
ninguno(a)(s) (none, not any, no)	alguno(a)(s) (some)
ni . . . ni (neither, nor)	o . . . o (either, or)
tampoco (neither, not either)	también (also)
todavía no (not yet)	ya (already)
ya no (no longer)	todavía (still)

Notes.

1. If a negative word other than **no** precedes the verb, it may stand alone. If the negative word follows the verb, **no** must precede the verb.

   Nadie viene.   No viene nadie.

   Nunca voy al desierto.   No voy nunca al desierto.

2. Unlike English, Spanish uses double and triple negatives. In fact, an affirmative word should not follow a negative.

Nunca bebo ni café ni té.

Scrooge nunca da nada a nadie.

Exercise A. Change to the negative.

1. Puedo ir también.

   _____

2. Hay algo en la mesa.

   _____

3. Marisa tiene algunos juguetes (toys).

   _____

4. Vieron a alguien.

   _____

5. Voy a la biblioteca o al museo.

   _____

6. Siempre vamos al cine.

   _____

Exercise B. Translate the word in parentheses.

1. ¿Hay (something) en la caja (box)?   _____

2. Ellos no fueron a Europa (either).   _____

3. Bárbara (no longer) vive con sus
   padres.   _____

4. Hoy no tengo (either) lápiz (or) pluma.   _____

5. No conocemos a (anyone) aquí.   _____

6. ¿Hay (someone) a la puerta?   _____

7. (No) profesor sabe todo.   _____

8. (Some) día voy a volver a México.   _____

9. (No one) llegó a las seis.   _____

Exercise C. Answer negatively.

1. ¿Siempre lees novelas románticas?   _____

2. ¿Invitó Ud. a alguien al baile?   _____

3. ¿Escribiste algo en el cuaderno?   _____

4. ¿Viajas a España o a México?   _____

5. ¿Van Uds. a estudiar también?   _____

Exercise D. Translate into Spanish.

1. We don't speak Portuguese either.

   _____

2. He didn't see anyone.

   _____

3. She didn't bring anything to the party.

   _____

4. They never study in August.

   _____

5. Is there someone in the kitchen?

   _____

SECTION I   **A. Fill in with the correct form of ser or estar in the present tense.**

1. Mi padre _____ enfermo hoy.
2. Nosotros _____ mexicanos.
3. Ella _____ una mujer inteligente.
4. _____ tu amigo en la oficina?
5. Su caballo _____ en el rancho.
6. Mi casa _____ pequeña.
7. El agua _____ caliente.
8. Hoy _____ el catorce de febrero.
9. Ellas _____ de Nicaragua.
10. Mi gato _____ blanco y negro.

B. Rewrite the sentence replacing the noun (in italics) with an object pronoun (direct or indirect).

Model: Juan tiene *el libro*. Juan lo tiene.

1. Usted escribe *la carta* a María.   _____
2. Carlos manda el dinero a *sus padres*.   _____
3. Yo hablo a *María*.   _____
4. Yo veo a *Carmen*.   _____
5. Quiero mandar *el paquete*.   _____

C. Translate using a form of the verb gustar.

1. He likes them.

   _____

2. Do you (tú) like my dog?

   _____

3. We didn't like those buildings.

   _____

4. They like to eat enchiladas.

_____

5. I like Juan's sister.

_____

SECTION II A. Write the following verbs in the present tense.

1. traer: (yo)   _____
2. comenzar: tú   _____
3. despertarse: ellos   _____
4. querer: (ella)   _____
5. decir: yo   _____
6. mirar: nosotros   _____
7. oír: él   _____
8. escuchar: vosotros   _____
9. comer: nosotros   _____
10. hacer: yo   _____

B. Change from the present to the preterite.

1. llueve   _____
2. entiendo   _____
3. comprendes   _____
4. cierran   _____
5. vendemos   _____
6. recuerdan   _____
7. volvéis   _____
8. pierdes   _____
9. abre   _____
10. hablan   _____

C. Translate.

1. ¿Qué hacías cuando te llamé?

_____

2. ¿Sabían ustedes que él llegó esta mañana?

_____

3. Íbamos a salir temprano pero tuvimos mucho trabajo.

_____

4. ¿Qué decía ella? No oí.

_____

5. Ella se levantó tarde porque estaba cansada.

_____

MORE ON ADJECTIVES AND ADVERBS

DEMONSTRATIVE ADJECTIVES

Set 1	this	these	Examples	
fem.	esta	estas	esta casa	estas casas
masc.	este	estos	este libro	estos libros

Set 2	that	those	Examples	
fem.	esa	esas	esa mesa	esas mesas
masc.	ese	esos	ese gato	esos gatos

Set 3	that	those	Examples	
fem.	aquella	aquellas	aquella cosa	aquellas cosas
masc.	aquel	aquellos	aquel día	aquellos días

Note. Remember from the discussion of demonstrative pronouns in Chapter 12 that space and time are divided into three units according to the distance between the speaker and the object. Set 3 refers to things that are farther removed than Set 2 (that is, Set 3 would be "those over there").

Exercise A. Translate the word indicated. (The "aquel" series should be used with "over there" and "long ago.")

1. Quiero (this) vestido, por favor.   _____

2. ¿Puedes ver (that, over there) montaña?   _____

3. Necesitamos (those) tijeras (scissors).   _____

4. Voy a dar (these) revistas a Lorena.   _____

5. Yo vivía en Lima en (that, long ago) año.   _____

6. Antonio va a comprar (that) coche.   _____

7. No me gustan (these) frijoles (beans, masc.).   _____

8. Los pájaros viven en (those, over there) árboles.   _____

9. (That) hombre es demasiado guapo.   _____

10. (These) mujeres son mis amigas.   _____

SHORTENED FORMS OF ADJECTIVES

The following words drop the final -o when they precede a masculine singular noun.

uno	un hombre
bueno	un buen muchacho
malo	un mal libro
primero	el primer día
tercero	el tercer curso
alguno	algún día
ninguno	ningún presidente

Notes.

1. **Ciento (100)** shortens to **cien** before nouns and before **mil** and **millones.** It remains **ciento** with other numerals.

cien personas	100 people
cien mil animales	100,000 animals
ciento ochenta libras	180 pounds

2. **Grande** *shortens to* **gran** before a singular noun. The meaning in this position changes from "large" to "great."

El fue un gran rey.	He was a great king.
Ella es una gran artista.	She is a great artist.

3. **Santo** *becomes* **San** before masculine singular names, except those beginning with To- or Do-.

   San José   San Juan   Santo Domingo   Santo Tomás

4. **Cualquiera** (any) becomes **cualquier** before a noun.

   cualquier estudiante

   cualquier pluma

Exercise B. Translate the word in parentheses.

1. Marzo es el (third) mes del año.   _____
2. Hizo el (first) ejercicio.   _____
3. (Saint) Pedro y (Saint) Diego son santos famosos.   _____
4. Roma es una (great) ciudad.   _____
5. Es un (good) día para ir a las montañas.   _____
6. Gerardo está de (bad) humor hoy.   _____
7. No hay (no) modo de resolver el problema.   _____

COMPARATIVES AND SUPERLATIVES

Superiority	=	más + noun + que
Inferiority	=	menos + noun + que
Equality/inequality	=	tanto(s),-a(s) + noun + como

With Nouns

Pedro tiene más zapatos que Carlos.
(Peter has more shoes than Charles.)

Carlos no tiene tantos zapatos como Pedro.
(Charles doesn't have as many shoes as Peter.)

Note. The comparative form of **bueno** is **mejor** (better) and the comparative form of **malo** is **peor** (worse). The superlatives for these are:

The Best	**The Worst**
el (la) mejor	el (la) peor
los (las) mejores	los (las) peores

With Adjectives and Adverbs

Superiority	=	más + adjective or adverb + que
Inferiority	=	menos + adjective or adverb + que
Equality/inequality	=	tan + adjective or adverb + como

Mi perro es más inteligente que tu perro.
(My dog is more intelligent than your dog.)

Tu perro es menos inteligente que mi perro.
(Your dog is less intelligent than my dog.)

Tu perro no es tan inteligente como el mio.
(Your dog is not as intelligent as mine.)

-ísmo

The affix -ísmo is an absolute superlative meaning "to a very high degree." The superlative is formed by adding -ísimo (-a, -os, -as) to an adjective and -ísimamente to an adverb (for example, **rápidamente** becomes **rapidísimamente**).

Exercise C. Translate.

1. Jaime is taller than his father.

   _____

2. I have more records than Teodoro.

   _____

3. The cat is not as big as the dog.

   _____

4. I am as busy (ocupado) as Mr. Romero.

   _____

5. They buy as many flowers as Ana (does — not expressed).

   _____

6. The coffee is better than the tea.

   _____

7. The hamburgers (hamburguesas) in the cafeteria are bad, but the enchiladas are worse.

   _____

NOMINALIZING ADJECTIVES

un joven	a young man	lo malo	the bad part
la pobre	the poor woman	lo bueno	the good part

Notes.

1. An adjective that refers to a person may be used as a noun when preceded by an indefinite or definite article.

2. A masculine singular adjective preceded by **lo** functions as an abstract noun.

3. The expression **a lo mejor** is an idiomatic expression meaning "probably."

Exercise D. Translate the words in parentheses.

1. (The interesting part) es que ellos se casaron. _____

2. ¿Conoces a aquella (blond woman)? _____

3. Me gusta más (the little one). _____

4. (The rich) no sufren como los pobres. _____

5. ¿Qué muchacho? ¿(The tall one)? _____

USING PAST PARTICIPLES TO FORM ADJECTIVES

An adjective in the masculine singular form, in many cases, is the same as the past participle of the verb. The past participle is formed by taking the stem of the infinitive and adding -ado for -ar infinitives and -ido for -er and -ir infinitives.

Infinitive	Past Participle (never changes)	Adjective (agrees with noun)
cerrar	cerrado	cerrado (closed)
conocer	conocido	conocido (known)
recibir	recibido	recibido (received)

Some common irregular past participles and corresponding adjectives are:

hacer	hecho (made/done)
escribir	escrito (written)
abrir	abierto (open)
morir	muerto (dead)
decir	dicho (said)

Note. See Chapter 27 for a discussion of how past participles are used in compound tenses.

Exercise E. Translate the adjective. Be sure it agrees with the noun it modifies.

1. Las ventanas están (open). _____

2. La maleta está bien (made). _____

3. Julio Cortázar es un autor bien (known). _____

4. La comida ya está (prepared). _____

5. ¿Están bien (written) las cartas? _____

6. Es domingo y el banco está (closed). _____

MAKING AN ADVERB

An adverb is formed by taking the feminine singular form of an adjective and adding -mente, the equivalent of "-ly."

rápida + mente = rápidamente (rapidly)

fácil + mente = fácilmente (easily)

inteligente + mente = inteligentemente (intelligently)

Note. In some cases, the feminine form of the adjective is the same as the masculine form (for example, **fácil, inteligente**).

Exercise F. Write the adverb for the following adjectives and translate into English.

1. fácil   fácilmente   easily
2. lento   _____
3. probable   _____
4. rápido   _____
5. alegre   _____
6. claro   _____
7. real   _____
8. necesario   _____
9. completo   _____
10. posible   _____

Exercise G. Complete the sentences with the adverb derived from the adjective in parentheses.

1. Los alumnos trabajan (diligente) cada día. _____

2. El contesta (correcto) en español. _____

3. (General) comen a las dos en Madrid. _____

4. Tiene que salir del país (inmediato). _____

5. (Final) llegó la carta esperada. _____

6. Nuestro candidato puede ganar la elección (fácil). _____

7. Cantas esa canción (perfecto). _____

8. Vamos a Nueva York (frecuente). _____

FORMAL COMMANDS (THE IMPERATIVE)

Formal commands are those you use when you address a person as **usted** or a group of people as **ustedes**.

Tráigame una copa de vino, por favor.	Bring me a glass of wine, please.
Dígame su nombre, señorita.	Tell me your name, Miss.
No hagan eso, por favor.	Don't do that, please.

Notes.

1. The formal command is formed by taking the **yo** form of the present tense (except for verbs ending in -oy).

Infinitive	First Person
traer	traigo
decir	digo
hacer	hago
recordar	recuerdo

Then take off the -o ending and add -a to stems whose infinitives end in -er or -ir and -e to stems whose infinitives end in -ar.

traig + a = traiga
dig + a = diga
hag + a = haga
recuerd + e = recuerde

Add -n for the **ustedes** form.

traigan
digan
hagan
recuerden

2. The following verbs have irregular commands:

ir	vaya/n	estar	esté/n
dar	de/n	saber	sepa/n
ser	sea/n		

3. Object and reflexive pronouns are attached to an affirmative command. A written accent is needed on the stressed syllable.

Cánteme la canción.	Cántemela.
Tráiganos la cuenta.	Tráiganosla.
Levántense temprano.	

4. Object and reflexive pronouns precede a negative command.

No me lo dé hasta mañana.

No se vaya ahora.

5. Two types of spelling changes occur with certain verbs. Just as with the preterite, verbs that end in -car change to -que and -quen to maintain the [k] sound.

tocar	toque Ud.	toquen Uds.
buscar	busque Ud.	busquen Uds.

Verbs that end in -gar insert a "u" before the "e" to maintain the [g].

pagar	pague Ud.	paguen Uds.
llegar	llegue Ud.	lleguen Uds.

Exercise A. Write the formal commands for the following verbs.

Infinitive	First Person	Singular	Plural
Model: contar	cuento	cuente	cuenten
1. tener	_____	_____	_____
2. cerrar	_____	_____	_____
3. volver	_____	_____	_____
4. oír	_____	_____	_____
5. aprender	_____	_____	_____
6. venir	_____	_____	_____
7. poner	_____	_____	_____
8. leer	_____	_____	_____
9. dormir	_____	_____	_____
10. repetir	_____	_____	_____

Exercise B. Write the imperative of the following verbs.

1. (Abrir) Ud. la puerta, por favor.   _____
2. No (traducir) Uds. las frases ahora.   _____

3. (Pensar) Ud. en sus padres. _____

4. No (escribir) Uds. en la mesa. _____

5. (Mandar) Ud. el dinero inmediatamente. _____

6. (Traer) Uds. los refrescos. _____

7. (Ser) Ud. honesto. _____

8. No (conducir) Ud. tan rápidamente. _____

9. (Ir) Uds. con ellos. _____

10. (Dar) Ud. esta carta a Elena, por favor. _____

Exercise C. Answer the questions as shown in the model.

Model: ¿Digo el chiste (Shall I tell the joke)?

Sí, dígalo.   No, no lo diga.

1. ¿Sirvo la cena?

_____

2. ¿Hago los ejercicios?

_____

3. ¿Cierro la puerta?

_____

4. ¿Como el helado (ice cream)?

_____

5. ¿Doy la manzana (apple) al caballo?

_____

Exercise D. Answer as shown in the model.

Model: ¿Conducimos el coche?

Sí, condúzcanlo.   No, no lo conduzcan.

1. ¿Buscamos a Juan?

_____

2. ¿Compramos el sofá?

_____

3. ¿Comemos el pescado?

_____

4. ¿Limpiamos la casa?

_____

5. ¿Cocinamos (cook) las patatas?

_____

23

FUTURE AND CONDITIONAL TENSES

References to future action may be expressed in several ways in Spanish. The simple present tense is frequently used to refer to the immediate future (later today or tomorrow). The "going to + verb" form (known as the periphrastic future) may be used for near or distant future. The future tense itself may be used for any reference to future action. Here are examples of each possibility.

Te llamo más tarde.	I'll call you later.
Voy a comer temprano.	I'm going to eat early.
Llegarán mañana.	They will arrive tomorrow.

PERIPHRASTIC FUTURE: IR A WITH INFINITIVE

The future may be expressed with **ir a** and an infinitive, a structure that is parallel to "to be going to" in English.

¿Qué vas a hacer mañana?	What are you going to do tomorrow?
Vamos a ver la película.	We're going to see the movie.

Note. Vamos a + verb may also be translated "let's + verb."

REGULAR FUTURE FORMS

Mirar

Person	Singular		Plural	
1st	(yo)	miraré	(nosotros, -as)	miraremos
2nd	(tú)	mirarás	(vosotros, -as)	miraréis
3rd	(Ud., él, ella)	mirará	(Uds., ellos, -as)	mirarán

Leer

Person	Singular		Plural	
1st	(yo)	leeré	(nosotros, -as)	leeremos
2nd	(tú)	leerás	(vosotros, -as)	leeréis
3rd	(Ud., él, ella)	leerá	(Uds., ellos, -as)	leerán

Notes.

1. The future tense is formed by taking the infinitive and adding the following endings: -é, -ás, -á, -emos, -éis, -án.

2. The future tense is also used to express probability in the present. It may express "wonder," when we are looking for an answer to something.

¿Dónde estará mi hermano?	I wonder where my brother is. (Where can he be?)
Estará en casa de David.	He's probably at David's house.
¿Qué hora será?	I wonder what time it is.
Serán las cinco.	It's probably five o'clock.

Exercise A. Fill in the blank with the correct form of the verb in the future tense.

1. Juan (estar) en los Estados Unidos dos semanas.   _____
2. ¿Cuándo (volver) tus padres de Europa?   _____
3. Pienso que ellos (ir) a París en el verano.   _____
4. El avión (llegar) a las diez.   _____
5. Yo (terminar) el proyecto después de las vacaciones.   _____
6. ¿(Vestirse) tú en seguida (right away)?   _____
7. Nosotros (ver) a la familia Martín en México.   _____
8. Vosotros (cenar) con ellos mañana, ¿verdad?   _____

Exercise B. Change from the ir plus infinitive form to the future.

Model: Voy a tomar jugo. Tomaré jugo.

1. Voy a escribir una novela.   _____
2. Vamos a vender las casa.   _____
3. ¿Cuándo vas a terminar la tarea?   _____
4. Voy a descansar (to rest) todo el día.   _____
5. Van a vivir en Guatemala.   _____

IRREGULAR FUTURE

The few verbs that are irregular in the future can be classified into three types.

First Type: Drop "e" from the Infinitive Ending

querer — querré, querrás, querrá, querremos, querréis, querrán

caber — cabré, cabrás, cabrá, cabremos, cabréis, cabrán

poder — podré, podrás, podrá, podremos, podréis, podrán

saber — sabré, sabrás, sabrá, sabremos, sabréis, sabrán

haber — habré, habrás, habrá, habremos, habréis, habrán

Note. The infinitive **haber** gives us the present tense verb **hay** (there is, there are) and functions as the auxiliary verb in compound structures (see Chapter 27).

Examples.

¿Cúando sabrás?	When will you know?
Habrá mucha gente en la playa.	There will be a lot of people on the beach.
No podremos terminar hasta el lunes.	We will not be able to finish until Monday.

Second Type: "d" Replaces "e"

poner — pondré, pondrás, pondrá, pondremos, pondréís, pondrán

salir — saldré, saldrás, saldrá, saldremos, saldréis, saldrán

tener — tendré, tendrás, tendrá, tendremos, tendréís, tendrán

valer — valdré, valdrás, valdrá, valdremos, valdréis, valdrán

venir — vendré, vendrás, vendrá, vendremos, vendréis, vendrán

Examples.

Pondré mi dinero en el banco.	I'll put my money in the bank.
Saldremos el domingo a las tres.	We'll leave Sunday at three.
¿Cuánto valdrá la pintura?	I wonder how much the painting is worth. (Remember the future is used to express wondering and probability.)

Third Type: Stem Change

decir — diré, dirás, dirá, diremos, diréis, dirán

hacer — haré, harás, hará, haremos, haréis, harán

Examples.

Ellos me dirán la respuesta.	They will tell me the answer.
¿Qué haremos si llueve?	What will we do if it rains?

Note. Few verbs are irregular in the future tense. The previous verbs have irregular stems, but the endings are regular.

Exercise C. Change from the present to the future.

1. Tenemos que esperar hasta las cuatro. _____
2. Usted puede volver mañana. _____
3. ¿Cuánto valen las joyas? _____
4. Mi papá sale para Londres el lunes. _____
5. ¿A qué hora vienes? _____
6. Yo no sé los resultados de los examenes. _____
7. ¿Dónde ponen Uds. los libros? _____
8. ¿Cabemos todos en el mismo coche? _____
9. El dice la verdad. _____
10. No quieren ir. _____

THE CONDITIONAL TENSE

The conditional is expressed in English with "would." The conditional is to the past what the future is to the present. Note the following:

		Present/Future
She says she will be here.		Dice que estará aquí.
		Past/Conditional
She said she would be here.		Dijo que estaría aquí.

Person		Hablar	Comer	Vivir
1st	(yo)	hablaría	comería	viviría
2nd	(tú)	hablarías	comerías	vivirías
3rd	(Ud., el, ella)	hablaría	comería	viviría
1st	(nosotros, -as)	hablaríamos	comeríamos	viviríamos
2nd	(vosotroa, -as)	hablaríais	comeríais	vivirías
3rd	(Uds., ellos, -as)	hablarían	comerían	vivirían

Notes.

1. The conditional is formed by taking the entire infinitive and adding the following endings: -ía, -ías, -ía, -íamos, -íais, -ían. The endings are the same as those used to form the imperfect.

2. The same verbs that are irregular in the future are irregular in the conditional. Use the future bases you learned and add the conditional endings. Here are examples of each of the three types:

   querer — querría, querrías, querría, querríamos, querríais, querrían

   tener — tendría, tendrías, tendría, tendríamos, tendríais, tendrían

   decir — diría, dirías, diría, diríamos, diríais, dirían

3. The conditional may be used to indicate probability in the past. It may also be used to express wonder related to something in the past. This usage is parallel to the use of the future to express probability and wonder in the present.

¿Dónde estaría el gato?	I wonder where the cat was.
Estaría en el garage.	He was probably in the garage.

Exercise D. Fill in the blank with the correct form of the verb in the conditional.

1. ¿(Correr) tú diez millas?   _____
2. ¿Qué (buscar) ellos?   _____
3. Ella (traducir) la lectura.   _____
4. Nosotros (volver) antes de las ocho.   _____
5. Mi amigo (ayudar) con el coche.   _____
6. ¿Adónde (ir) tú en la primavera?   _____
7. Yo no (escoger) ese (that) restaurante.   _____
8. Juan prometió que me (visitar) mañana.   _____

Exercise E. Change to the conditional.

1. ¿Quiere Ud. dar dinero a su amigo? _____
2. Todos los libros no caben aquí. _____
3. Yo hago la limpieza (cleaning) pero no tengo tiempo. _____
4. Nosotros venimos solos. _____
5. El cuadro (picture) vale muchísimo. _____
6. El puede regresar a las nueve. _____
7. Ellos no tienen que llamar. _____
8. ¿Salís el miércoles entonces? _____
9. Pongo todo el dinero en el banco. _____
10. ¿Me dices el secreto? _____

Exercise F. Change from the present to the future and conditional.

Present	Future	Conditional
1. escribo	_____	_____
2. repite	_____	_____
3. haces	_____	_____
4. se acuesta	_____	_____
5. tienen	_____	_____
6. hay (haber)	_____	_____
7. puedo	_____	_____
8. sabemos	_____	_____
9. dices	_____	_____
10. vende	_____	_____

Exercise G. Translate into Spanish.

1. (We will sleep) hasta las once.

_____

2. Ella (would prepare) toda la comida.

_____

3. (It is probably) las nueve y media.

_____

4. (There will be) un baile el viernes.

_____

5. (I would like) ganar la lotería.

_____

6. Olga Martinez Campos (was probably) sick.

_____

7. Su esposa (is probably) unos cincuenta años.

   _____

8. (They would leave) después de nosotros.

   _____

9. (I will not drive) en Boston.

   _____

10. (He probably did) el trabajo.

    _____

FAMILIAR COMMANDS (IMPERATIVE)

REGULAR VERBS

Singular (Tú) Commands

Affirmative

hablar	Habla.	Speak.
beber	Bebe.	Drink.
escribir	Escribe.	Write.

Negative

hablar	No hables.	Don't speak.
beber	No bebas.	Don't drink.
escribir	No escribas.	Don't write.

Plural (Vosotros) Commands

Affirmative

hablar	Hablad.	Speak.
beber	Bebed.	Drink.
escribir	Escribid.	Write.

Negative

hablar	No habléis.	Don't speak.
beber	No bebáis.	Don't drink.
comer	No comáis.	Don't eat.

Notes.

1. The affirmative **tú** command is the same as the third person singular of the present indicative. The pronoun **tú** is generally omitted.

2. The affirmative **vosotros** command is formed by dropping the -r of the infinitive and replacing it with -d.

3. The rules for using object pronouns and reflexive pronouns are the same for the familiar commands as they are for the formal commands. See Chapter 22.

Dímelo ahora, por favor.   Tell it to me now, please.
No me digas.   Don't tell me.
Escribidlo hoy.   Write it today.
No lo escribáis mañana.   Don't write it tomorrow.

IRREGULAR VERBS (TÚ ONLY)

Irregular familiar commands occur in the singular only. The **vosotros** forms, which are used by a small percentage of the Spanish-speaking world, are regular.

Infinitive	Affirmative	Negative
decir	di	no digas
hacer	haz	no hagas
ir	ve	no vayas
poner	pon	no pongas
salir	sal	no salgas
ser	sé	no seas
tener	ten	no tengas
valer	val	no valgas
venir	ven	no vengas

Exercise A. Change to commands.

Model: tú duermes: duerme

1. tú das _____
2. tú no vuelves _____
3. vosotros coméis _____
4. vosotros no habláis _____
5. tú haces _____
6. tú no lees _____
7. tú sales _____
8. vosotros estudiáis _____
9. tú no cantas _____
10. tú pones

Exercise B. Change to the command form as indicated, as though each item were a dialogue.

Model: ¿Leo este capítulo? Sí, _____

(Shall I read this chapter?) Sí, léelo, por favor.

¿Lo hagamos ahora? No, _____

(Shall we do it now?) No, no lo hagáis.

1. ¿Salimos a la una? Sí, _____
2. ¿Traigo el postre? Sí, _____
3. ¿Bailamos el tango? No, _____

4. ¿Vengo mañana? Sí, _____

5. ¿Hago el viaje? No, _____

6. ¿Escribimos la carta? Sí, _____

7. ¿Digo la verdad? Sí, _____

8. ¿Como el plátano? No, _____

VERBS REQUIRING A PREPOSITION BEFORE AN INFINITIVE; SPECIAL USES OF INFINITIVES

VERBS THAT REQUIRE A PREPOSITION BEFORE INFINITIVES

Verbs of motion, as well as some other verbs, require the preposition **"a"** after the conjugated verb and before an infinitive. Study the following examples.

Vamos a salir mañana.	We're going to leave tomorrow.
Juan viene a comer conmigo.	Juan's coming to eat with me.
Ella aprende a esquiar.	She learns to ski.

Common Verbs Requiring "a" Before an Infinitive

acostumbrarse a	to get accustomed to
aprender a	to learn to
atreverse a	to dare to
ayudar a	to help to
empezar a	to begin to
enseñar a	to teach to
invitar a	to invite to
ir a	to be going to
llegar a	to succeed in, arrive at
negarse a	to refuse to
salir a	to go out to
subir a	to go up to
tender a	to tend to
venir a	to come to
volver a	to do again, return to

Common Verbs Requiring "de" Before an Infinitive

acabar de	to have just (plus past participle)
acordarse de	to remember to
alegrarse de	to be glad to
avisar de	to warn to
culpar de	to blame for
deber de	must
dejar de	to stop (doing something)
desfrutar de	to enjoy
gozar de	to enjoy
hartarse de	to be fed up with
ocuparse de	to take care of
olvidarse de	to forget to
reírse de	to laugh about
tratar de	to try to
tratarse de	to be a question of

Exercise A. Fill in the blank with "a" or "de."

1. Mis amigos acaban _____ llegar.
2. Juan nos puede ayudar _____ terminar el trabajo.
3. No quiero dejar _____ estudiar el español.
4. Chela se alegra _____ ver a su primo.
5. Yo me harto _____ limpiar la casa.
6. La maestra les enseña _____ los niños a leer.
7. ¿Te acordaste _____ cerrar la puerta?
8. Mis amigos me invitaron _____ comer con ellos.
9. Ella no se atreva _____ ir en avion.
10. El niño se negó _____ acostarse temprano.

SPECIAL USES OF INFINITIVES

Unlike English, Spanish uses an infinitive after a preposition. In English, the present participle is generally used.

Después de comer, fuimos al cine.	After eating, we went to the movies.
Joaquín estudió los mapas antes de hacer el viaje.	Joaquin studied the maps before taking the trip.
Estudiamos para aprender.	We study in order to learn.
Al llegar, Sarita dio un regalo a su prima.	Upon arriving, Sarita gave a gift to her cousin.

Note. Al + an infinitive is translated as "upon" plus the present participle of the verb or "when" plus a conjugated verb.

Exercise B. Translate.

1. Antes de salir, Vicente pagó la cuenta.

_____

2. Comemos para vivir.

_____

3. Vamos a ir la playa después de cenar.

_____

POR/PARA AND PERO/SINO

POR VERSUS PARA

In many cases, **para** looks ahead to a destination or purpose and **por** looks back to a cause.

Para

Escribí la carta para Juan.	I wrote the letter for John. (John will receive it.)

Por

Escribí la carta por Juan.	I wrote the letter for John. (He couldn't do it, so I did it for him.)

Para

Estudiarás para salir bien en el examen.	You will study in order to do well on the exam.

Por

Saliste mal en el examen por no estudiar.	You did badly on the exam because you didn't study. (Because of not studying.)

SPECIFIC USES OF PARA

1. Destination.

Mañana salimos para África.	Tomorrow we're leaving for Africa.
Estas flores son para usted.	These flowers are for you.

2. Deadline or date.

Necesito el libro para mañana.	I need the book by tomorrow.
Mi cita con el dentista es para el lunes.	My appointment with the dentist is for Monday.

3. The purpose of an object.

una caja para cigarros	a cigar box

una taza para café   a coffee cup

una casa para perros   a dog house

4. Comparison of inequality (that is, in spite of).

Es muy maduro para un niño.   He's very mature for a child.

Lo hace bien para un principiante   He does it well for a beginner.

5. **Estar para** + infinitive means "to be about to."

Estamos para comprar una casa.   We're about to buy a house.

¿Crees que está para llover?   Do you think it's about to rain?

6. **Para** may be used with a profession to indicate a career goal.

Estudio para abogado.   I'm studying to be a lawyer.

SPECIFIC USES OF POR

1. As an agent (by).

Guernica fue pintada por Picasso.   Guernica was painted by Picasso.

2. In time expressions indicating duration.

Estaremos allí por dos meses.   We'll be there for two months.

Bailaron por una hora.   They danced for an hour.

3. **Estar** + **por** means "to be in favor of"; **estar por** + **infinitive** means "to be inclined to" or "in the mood to."

Estamos por los Dodgers.   We're for the Dodgers.

Estamos por quedarnos.   We're in the mood to stay.

4. **Por** is used to express manner or motive.

Vamos por avión.   We go by plane.

Lo mandé por correo aereo.   I sent it air mail.

Lo hizo por amor.   He did it for (because of) love.

5. **Por** expresses "in exchange for."

Te daremos cinco dólares por los discos.   We'll give you ten dollars for the records.

6. **Por** is used to indicate measure or velocity.

El límite de velocidad es 55 millas por hora.   The speed limit is 55 miles per hour.

7. **Por** expresses estimation or opinion.

Jenny pasaría por española.   Jenny would pass as (for) a Spaniard.

8. **Por** may express an indefinite place or time.

¿Hay árboles por allí?   Are there trees around there?

Exercise A. Fill in the blank with por or para.

1. Rosa compro la blusa _____ dos mil pesetas.
2. Si es posible, prefiero tener mis clases _____ la mañana.
3. Antonio Pérez es muy activo _____ su edad.
4. No me gusta viajar _____ avión.
5. María compró el reloj _____ su padre.
6. Estuvieron en México _____ un mes.
7. Escribieron una composición _____ mañana.
8. Anoche se pasearon _____ la playa.
9. Lo siento pero _____ aquí no hay restaurantes.
10. Muchos soldados murieron _____ su patria en la última guerra.
11. Salen _____ Caracas el mes que viene.
12. Lisa se puso enferma y su amiga trabajo _____ ella.
13. ¿Terminarás el cuento _____ el viernes?
14. Este regalo es _____ ti.
15. Rafael piensa estudiar _____ médico.
16. Irá a la tienda _____ pan.
17. _____ estar cansado después de esquiar, Juan no salió bien en su examen.
18. _____ favor, prepare Ud. este diálogo _____ el jueves.
19. No fue al baile _____ falta de ropa.
20. Conducía su coche a una velocidad de 60 millas _____ hora.

Exercise B. Translate the words in parentheses into Spanish.

1. He viajado (throughout) toda Europa.   _____
2. (For) un estudiante perezoso, Miguel recibe buenas notas.   _____
3. Luisa estudia (in order to be) intérprete de lenguas.   _____
4. Cristina va a tener el trabajo terminado (by) el viernes.   _____
5. Juan (is about to) salir porque tiene una cita.   _____
6. Mi madre me mandó a la librería (for) un libro.   _____
7. Yo tuve que pagar cinco dólares (for) aquel libro.   _____

8. (On account of) falta de dinero, no fuimos al _____
   cine.

9. Pagaron cien dólares (per) semana.   _____

10. Pasaron (along) la playa.   _____

PERO VERSUS SINO

Both **pero** and **sino** mean "but." However, **sino** is used only when the first clause of the sentence is negative, and the second clause is in direct contrast. It may generally be translated "but rather." **Sino que** is used when the clause introduces a new verb.

Juan no es gordo, sino delgado (thin).	John isn't fat, but rather he's thin.
El café no es bueno, sino horrible.	The coffee isn't good but rather it's horrible.
Pepito no terminó el trabajo, sino que lo dejó y fue al cine.	Pepito didn't finish the work, but rather he left it and went to the movies.
Mi coche no es elegante pero es económico.	My car isn't elegant, but it's economical.

Note. The English translation "but rather" may seem awkward. For a smoother translation, drop the "but rather" and use a semicolon between the two clauses.

Exercise C. Fill in the blank with pero or sino.

1. Tu coche es muy elegante _____ caro (expensive).

2. Ellos no viven aquí _____ en Miami.

3. No escribí a Antonio _____ a Jorge.

4. Él es pobre _____ muy bien educado.

5. Mi abuelo es viejo _____ muy activo.

6. No quiero ser escritor _____ actor.

7. Ella no toma vino tinto (red) _____ blanco.

8. Puedo ir mañana _____ no puedo ir el jueves.

9. No puedo ir el jueves _____ mañana.

10. Marta no habla francés _____ italiano.

COMPOUND TENSES WITH HABER (PERFECT TENSES)

The perfect tenses are compound verbs that have a form of the auxiliary verb "to have" (haber) and the past participle of the main verb. The auxiliary verb can be put into different tenses.

PRESENT PERFECT TENSE

The present perfect tense, a combination of **haber** in the present tense and the past participle of any verb, is used to describe the recent past.

Hemos comido bien hoy.	We have eaten well today.
¿Has hablado con ella?	Have you talked with her?
No han almorzado todavía.	They haven't had lunch yet.

Haber (to Have — Auxiliary)

Person	Singular		Plural	
1st	(yo)	he	(nosotros, -as)	hemos
2nd	(tú)	has	(vosotros, -as)	habéis
3rd	(Ud., él, ella)	ha	(Uds., ellos -as)	han

Regular Past Participles

-ar:	llegar	llegado
-er:	comer	comido
-ir:	vivir	vivido

Irregular Past Participles			
abrir	abierto	imprimir	impreso
cubrir	cubierto	morir	muerto
decir	dicho	poner	puesto
descubrir	descubierto	resolver	resuelto
disolver	disuelto	romper	roto
envolver	envuelto	ver	visto
escribir	escrito	volver	vuelto
hacer	hecho		

Notes.

1. While English sometimes divides the present perfect construction, Spanish does not.

   Nunca he ido.   I have never gone.

   ¿Has ido tú?   Have you gone?

2. Spanish has two verbs, **haber** and **tener**, to the one English verb: "to have." The verb **tener** is not used to form compound tenses. It may, however, be used in the following construction in which **tener** is combined with an adjective.

Examples.

   ¿Has hecho el trabajo?   Have you done the work?

   Sí, lo he hecho.   Yes, I have done it.

   Lo tengo hecho.   I have it done.

   ¿Han abierto Uds. las   Have you opened the
   ventanas?   windows?

   Sí, las hemos abierto.   We have opened them.

   Las tenemos abiertas.   We have them open.

3. Past participles ending in -ido whose stems end in a vowel have an accent over the "i": **leído, caído, oído, creído.**

Exercise A. Write the past participle of the following verbs.

1. beber   _____   6. almorzar   _____
2. cantar   _____   7. aprender   _____
3. recibir   _____   8. sufrir   _____
4. llegar   _____   9. perder   _____
5. subir   _____   10. pedir   _____

Exercise B. Write the verb in the correct form of the present perfect.

1. Él (comer) en aquel restaurante.   _____
2. Uds. (trabajar) mucho hoy, ¿verdad?   _____

3. ¿(Abrir) tú los regalos de Navidad? _____

4. Yo no (leer) el periódico todavía. _____

5. Nosotros (romper) la botella. _____

6. Dónde (estar) vosotros esta tarde? _____

7. Ellos ya (salir) de casa. _____

8. ¿Quién te (decir) que no hay clase? _____

PLUPERFECT TENSE

The pluperfect is formed by using the imperfect tense of **haber** with the past participle.

Habíamos ido a la playa.	We had gone to the beach.
¿No habías practicado?	Hadn't you practiced?
Ellos no me habían dicho nada.	They hadn't said anything to me.

Exercise C. Write the correct form of the verb in the pluperfect.

1. Ellos (levantarse) muy tarde ayer. _____

2. Nosotros no le (escribir). _____

3. ¿(Vender) Uds. su casa? _____

4. Mi abuelo (morir) en Venezuela. _____

5. Yo nunca (oír) tal cosa. _____

6. Vosotros no lo (hacer). _____

7. ¿Dijo el profesor que ellos (descubrir) otra isla? _____

8. ¿(Poner) tú el dinero debajo del colchón (under the mattress)? _____

PRESENT PERFECT AND PLUPERFECT PROGRESSIVE TENSE

The present perfect progressive and pluperfect progressive tenses are formed by combining the appropriate form of **haber**, the present participle, and the past participle, as English does.

¿Has estado haciendo caso?	Have you been paying attention?
No he podido dormir porque él ha estado roncando.	I haven't been able to sleep because he's been snoring.
Habían estado hablando.	They had been talking.

Exercise D. Answer in Spanish using the progressive forms.

1. ¿Has estado trabajando en el jardín?

_____

2. ¿Han estado Uds. visitando a sus primos?

_____

3. ¿Qué has estado leyendo?

_____

4. ¿No habías estado viviendo en México?

   _____

5. ¿Han estado diciendo la verdad?

   _____

DIÁLOGO   **El Día Antes del Examen**

Alberto y Fernando hablan en la cafetería.

Alberto: ¿Has estudiado para el examen?

Fernando: Sí, mucho. Creo que sé todo.

Alberto: Yo no. He estado tan ocupado que todavía no he leído el último capítulo.

Fernando: Hombre, qué mala suerte. ¿Qué has estado haciendo?

Alberto: Pues, esta mañana tuve que llevar a mi perro al médico porque ha estado enfermo, y al salir de allí recordé que se me había olividado una cita con el dentista, y a la vez me di cuenta de que María me esperaba en el café.

Fernando: Tienes que organizar tu vida, Alberto.

Alberto: Es verdad. Ha sido un desastre últimamente.

Fernando: ¿Cuándo vas a prepararte para el examen?

Alberto: Después de comer. Tengo mucha hambre. ¿Has comido?

Fernando: No, todavía no. Voy a comer contigo y después podemos estudiar.

Exercise E. Preguntas sobre el diálogo.

1. ¿Quién no ha estudiado para el examen?

   _____

2. ¿Quién ya sabe todo?

   _____

3. ¿Qué ha estado haciendo Alberto?

   _____

4. ¿Por qué llevó Alberto su perro al médico?

   _____

5. ¿Qué quiere hacer Alberto antes de estudiar?

   _____

FUTURE PERFECT TENSE

The future perfect is formed by combining the future form of **haber** with the past participle. It is used to express an action that will take place by a certain time or prior to another future action.

Future of Haber Plus Past Participle

habré	habremos
habrás	habráis
habrá	habrán

} + past participle

Lo habré terminado para mañana.	I will have finished it by tomorrow.
¿Ya habrás ido?	Will you already have gone?

Exercise F. Write the correct form of the verb in the future perfect.

1. Yo (vivir) en España. _____
2. Él (terminar) la composición para el viernes. _____
3. Ellos lo (ver) antes de salir. _____
4. Nosotros (visitar) la Alhambra. _____
5. ¿(Volver) tú para las seis? _____
6. Vosotros (decidir) ir tambien. _____
7. ¿Lo (traer) ella esta vez? _____
8. Ellos (insistir), ¿verdad? _____

CONDITIONAL PERFECT

The conditional perfect ("would have" plus past participle) is formed by using the conditional form of the verb **haber** and the past participle. It is used to express an action that would have taken place (or would not have) if something else had not intervened.

Conditional of Haber Plus Past Participle

habría	habríamos
habrías	habríais
habría	habrían

} + past participle

Yo habría ido a Francia pero mi padre estaba enfermo.	I would have gone to France but my father was ill.
Te habría llamado pero mi teléfono estaba roto.	I would have called you but my phone was broken.

Exercise G. Write the correct form of the verb in the conditional perfect.

1. Vosotros (ir) a Guadalajara ayer, pero no había vuelo (flight). _____
2. ¿(Hacer) tú lo mismo que yo? _____
3. ¿Quién te (creer)? _____
4. Ellos no (poder) verlo. _____
5. Yo le (dar) ayuda. _____
6. Ella me lo (decir) pero tenía miedo. _____
7. Nosotros (acostarse) temprano. _____
8. ¿(Beber) ellos las dos botellas de vino? _____

Review Questions

Exercise H. Translate the words in parentheses into Spanish.

1. No sabían que yo le (had told) la verdad.   _____
2. (He has broken) todas las ventanas.   _____
3. (They have opened) una tienda nueva.   _____
4. ¿A qué hora (had begun) el concierto?   _____
5. Yo no (will have returned) para las cinco.   _____
6. Nosotros no (would have had) tiempo.   _____
7. Yo (have been) en Tijuana muchas veces.   _____
8. ¿(Will you have done) Uds. todo?   _____
9. Yo no (would have asked for) más dinero.   _____
10. Ellos (have not gotten dressed) todavía.   _____

PASSIVE VOICE

THE TRUE PASSIVE Many ideas can be expressed in both the active voice and the passive voice. To change an active sentence into a passive sentence, the direct object becomes the subject and the subject becomes an agent, generally introduced by the preposition **por**. The passive voice consists of a form of the verb **ser** and a past participle that agrees in number and gender with the noun it describes. Any tense may be used. Here are some examples of how to change an active sentence into a passive one.

Jaime escribe la carta.	James writes the letter.
La carta es escrita por Jaime.	The letter is written by James.
Julieta mandó los paquetes.	Juliet sent the packages.
Los paquetes fueron mandados por Julieta.	The packages were sent by Juliet.

Note. Spanish uses **ser** plus the past participle if the reference is to the happening of an action, but if the action is over and the result is referred to, then **estar** plus the past participle is used. "By" is usually translated **por**. However, if the past participle expresses opinion or emotion (for example, respected, feared) then **de** is generally used.

Exercise A. Change to the passive voice.

Model: Juan cerró las puertas.
              Las puertas fueron cerradas por Juan.

1. La criada preparó la comida.

   _____

2. Picasso pintó esos cuadros magníficos.

   _____

3. Julio ama a Concha.

   _____

4. El Sr. Rodriguez pagará las cuentas.

   _____

5. Los alumnos respetan a su profesora.

   _____

Exercise B. Translate the following expressions.

1. La Florida (was discovered by) Ponce de León.

   _____

2. El presidente (is respected by) todos.

   _____

3. Los ejercicios (were corrected by) los alumnos.

   _____

4. La cena (will be served by) mi hermana.

   _____

5. La ciudad (was destroyed by) el terremoto (earthquake).

   _____

THE PASSIVE USING SE

When an agent is not expressed, a reflexive construction is frequently used to express the passive.

Se habla español.	Spanish is spoken.
Se vive bien aquí.	One lives well here.
No se permite eso, hijito.	That is not allowed, son.
Las puertas se abren a las nueve.	The doors open at nine.

Note. Sometimes Spanish speakers use the third person plural, **ellos** (they), to express an indefinite subject. For example, "Robaron mi cartera" would be properly translated as "My wallet was stolen" when the subject is indefinite.

Exercise C. Change to the passive voice using "se."

Models: Cierran las puertas. (They close the doors.)
   Se cierran las puertas. (The doors were closed.)
   Abrieron la ventana. (They opened the window.)
   Se abrió la ventana. (The window was opened.)

1. Preparan los mariscos (shellfish).

   _____

2. Sirvieron la comida a las nueve.

   _____

3. Usaron madera (wood) para construir la casa.

   _____

4. Hablan francés en el Canadá.

   _____

5. No saben nada de su vida.

   _____

6. Vendieron las chaquetas a un precio bajo.

   _____

7. Anoche celebraron su cumpleaños.

_____

8. El año que viene producirán más café.

_____

Exercise D. Translate the following expressions, using "se."

1. ¿A qué hora (are opened) las tiendas el sábado?

_____

2. (People don't smoke much) en California.

_____

3. En este país (are spoken) inglés y español.

_____

4. ¿Cómo (does one say) "oven" en español?

_____

5. En los Estados Unidos (are sold) muchos zapatos españoles.

_____

6. (It is believed) que ellos son muy ricos.

_____

7. El año pasado no (were constructed) muchos edificios nuevos.

_____

8. Desde aquí (one can see) el centro de la ciudad.

_____

9. (They say) que ella vivió en esa casa por treinta años.

_____

10. A lo lejos (are heard) las campanas de la catedral.

_____

PRESENT SUBJUNCTIVE

All verb forms belong to one of several moods, or modes. So far we have seen just two moods: the indicative and the imperative. The indicative, used to express facts, is the most common mood used in English. The imperative is used to express a command (Chapters 22 and 24). The subjunctive is a subjective mood and generally indicates an attitude toward a statement. It may express desire, doubt, displeasure, or some other form of emotion. Let's see an example of each mood.

Indicative:

John drinks milk.   Juan bebe leche.

Imperative:

John, drink your milk.   Juan, bebe tu leche.

Subjunctive:

I prefer that John drink milk.   Prefiero que Juan beba leche.
(Not "drinks")

Note. In Spanish the subjunctive is widely used, but in English the subjunctive is restricted to the following few cases:

1. Expressing an impossible wish.

    I wish he were here.

        (Not "was")

2. Contrary-to-fact statements.

    I wouldn't say that if I were you.

        (Not "was")

3. In the dependent clause following a verb indicating a request, preference, or recommendation.

    We recommend that he go to Chicago.

        (Not "goes")

SUBJUNCTIVE FORMS

The present subjunctive is formed by taking the -o ending off the first person singular of the present indicative and adding the present subjunctive endings, which are roughly the reverse of those used for the indicative.

Regular Verbs

-ar: -e, -es, -e, -emos, -éis, -en
-er and **-ir:** -a, -as, -a, -amos, -áis, -an

Examples.

Person		Bailar	Volver	Decir	Cerrar
1st	(yo)	baile	vuelva	diga	cierre
2nd	(tú)	bailes	vuelvas	digas	cierres
3rd	(Ud., él, ella)	baile	vuelva	diga	cierre
1st	(nosotros, -as)	bailemos	volvamos	digamos	cerremos
2nd	(vosotros, -as)	bailéis	volváis	digáis	cerréis
3rd	(Uds., ellos, -as)	bailen	vuelvan	digan	cierran

Exercise A. Give the present subjunctive.

Model   poner: él _____

él ponga

1. traer: nosotros _____
2. hablar: Uds. _____
3. tener: tú _____
4. salir: ellos _____
5. esperar: yo _____
6. hacer: ella _____
7. entender: Ud. _____
8. perder: él _____

Irregular Verbs

The following five verbs are irregular in the present subjunctive.

Dar	Ir	Ser	Estar	Saber
dé	vaya	sea	esté	sepa
des	vayas	seas	estés	sepas
dé	vaya	sea	esté	sepa
demos	vayamos	seamos	estemos	sepamos
deis	vayáis	seáis	estéis	sepáis
den	vayan	sean	estén	sepan

THE SUBJUNCTIVE IN NOUN CLAUSES AND IMPERSONAL EXPRESSIONS

The subjunctive is used in sentences that have two parts: a main verb plus **que** and a noun clause. When the main verb tends to affect the course of what happens in the clause (to encourage or discourage, cause or prevent, etc.), and when there is a change of subject, the subjunctive is used in the noun clause.

Subject A: An Influence		Subject B: What Is Influenced
Yo quiero (I want	que that	tú me visites. you visit me.)
Ella prefiere (She prefers	que that	lo hagamos ahora. we do it now.)
Espero (I hope	que that	estén contentos. they are happy.)
Es necesario (It is necessary	que that	comas bien. you eat well.)

Notes.

1. When the dependent clause conveys information, the indicative is used, not the subjunctive.

   Ella sabe que voy.   She knows that I'm going.

   Veo que están contentos.   I see that they're happy.

2. When there is no change of subject, the indicative is used. The first verb is conjugated, and the following verb or verbs are in the infinitive form.

   Quiero ir.   I want to go.

   Quiero poder ir.   I want to be able to go.

   Es necesario ir.   It's necessary to go.

3. Change the structure of the English sentence to accommodate the Spanish before you translate.

   Example. I want you to bring it.
   I want that you bring it.
   Quiero que lo traigas.

4. Impersonal expressions that indicate certainty do not require the subjunctive.

   Es verdad que vienen mañana.

   Es evidente que ella está allí.

5. Common impersonal expressions that require the subjunctive are

Es dudoso que	It is doubtful that
Es importante que	It is important that
Es imposible que	It is impossible that
Es lástima que	It is a shame that
Es necesario que	It is necessary that
Es preciso que	It is necessary that

| Es posible que | It is possible that |
| Es probable que | It is probable (likely) that |

6. Common verbs that require the subjunctive in the noun clause, when there is a change of subject are, first, verbs of doubt or uncertainty:

| Dudamos que sea eso. | We doubt that it is that. |
| No estoy seguro que venga. | I'm not sure he's coming. |

Second, verbs indicating desire, indirect command (preference, request, and so on), prohibition, or advice also require the subjunctive.

Juan dice que le encontremos a las cinco.
John says for us to meet him at five.

El profesor no permite que lleguemos tarde.
The professor doesn't permit us to arrive late.

Te aconsejo que vayas temprano.
I advise you to go early.

Exercise B. Translate.

1. I doubt that they're here.

   _____

2. Do you want him to leave?

   _____

3. It is impossible for us to study today.

   _____

4. It's a shame she can't come.

   _____

5. I prefer to go early.

   _____

6. She's happy that it's sunny.

   _____

7. What does she want me to say?

   _____

WITH INDEFINITE OR NEGATIVE ANTECEDENTS

The subjunctive is also used in the following cases:

1. Adjective clauses with indefinite antecedents. When the speaker does not have a definite thing or things in mind to which his description applies, the verb of the clause is in the subjunctive.

   Come lo que (whatever) te guste, Juanito,
   Eat whatever you like, Juanito.

   Quiero una clase que sea divertida.
   I want a class that's fun.

2. Adjective clauses with negative antecedents.

No hay nadie que sepa.   There's no one who knows.

Exercise C. Choose the correct answer.

1. Busco una criada que (habla, hable) francés.   _____

2. Conozco a una mexicana que (entiende, entienda) perfectamente el inglés.   _____

3. ¿Hay alguien por aquí que (sabe, sepa) jugar el tenis?   _____

4. No conozco a nadie que lo (cree, crea) — dije an voz alta.   _____

5. Hay alguien aquí que me (quiere, quiera).   _____

6. Tenemos un apartamento que (esté, está) en la ciudad.   _____

7. Necesitan una secretaria que (sabe, sepa) taquigrafia.   _____

8. No hay ningún diccionario que (incluye, incluya) todas las palabras.   _____

9. Conozco a alguien que (pueda, puede) hacerlo.   _____

10. Tiene un vestido que (está, esté) muy de moda.   _____

Exercise D. Write the correct form of the verb.

1. Buscamos alguien que (hablar) tres lenguas.   _____

2. Viven en una casa que (tener) dos pisos.   _____

3. Queremos un regalo que (ser) bonito.   _____

4. Busco al chico que (tener) mi libro.   _____

5. ¿Conoces a alguien que (jugar) al fútbol profesional?   _____

6. No hay ningunas lámparas que me (gustar).   _____

7. Hay alguien en esta clase que (estar) enamorado (in love).   _____

8. No tienen nada que (valer) mucho.   _____

9. Busco un esposo que no (viajar) mucho.   _____

10. No hay nadie que me (dudar).   _____

IN ADVERBIAL CLAUSES Some conjunctions take the subjunctive, and some take the indicative. Others may take either, depending on the situation. The subjunctive deals with situations that are not regarded as factual or with things that have not yet happened. The indicative expresses factual things or situations that have occurred. Study the following charts.

Conjunctions That Take the Subjunctive

a menos que	unless
antes (de) que	before

con tal que	provided
para que	in order that, so that
sin que	without

Conjunctions That Take the Indicative

como	since, as
porque	because
pues	since, because
ya que	now that, since

Conjunctions That Take Either Subjunctive or Indicative

The following conjunctions take the subjunctive when the situation is something unknown, and the indicative when the situation is known.

aunque	although
como	as, the way
cuando	when
donde	where
según	according to what

Examples.

Aunque llueve, vamos.	Although it's raining, we're going.
Aunque llueva, vamos.	Although it may rain, we're going.
Cuando voy a París, visito los museos.	When (whenever) I go to Paris, I visit the museums.
Cuando vaya a París, visitaré los museos.	When I go to Paris (I haven't gone yet), I will visit the museums.

WITH QUIZÁS, TAL VEZ, AND OJALÁ

After **quizás** and **tal vez** (perhaps), the subjunctive is used when future time is implied. When present or past time is implied, either the subjunctive or the indicative may be used.

| Tal vez vayamos mañana. | Maybe we'll go tomorrow. |
| Quizá no vayan a venir. | Maybe they're not going to come. |

The subjunctive is always used after **ojalá** (from Arabic "wasala": May Allah grant). It is usually translated "I hope..." or "I wish...."

| Ojalá que tengamos buena suerte. | I hope we have good luck. |
| Ojalá que no fuera así. | I wish it weren't that way. |

Exercise E. Change to ojalá que and the subjunctive.

Model: Juan sabe. Ojalá que Juan sepa.

1. Él hace el trabajo.

2. Ellos están aquí.

   _____

3. Nosotros tenemos todo.

   _____

4. Usted sale bien en el examen.

   _____

5. Ella me dice el secreto.

   _____

6. Tú traes los discos.

   _____

DIÁLOGO

Rosita y su Papá

Rosita: ¿Puedo ir al cine esta tarde, Papá?

Papá: Quizás. Quiero que hagas tu trabajo primero. ¿Con quién vas?

Rosita: Con Paco.

Papá: ¿Paco? ¿El chico que conocí el otro día?

Rosita: No, ése fue Pedro. No creo que conozcas a Paco.

Papá: ¿Cómo conoces a Paco?

Rosita: De mi clase de historia. Es encantador. Papá, ¿qué trabajo quieres que haga?

Papá: Es necesario que limpies tu cuarto y cuando termines, puedes ir.

Rosita: Está bien, Papá. Y cuando llegue Paco, quiero que ustedes se conozcan.

IMPERFECT SUBJUNCTIVE

The imperfect subjunctive is used when the subjunctive mood is required and when the verb in the main clause is in the conditional or in a past tense.

IMPERFECT SUBJUNCTIVE FORMS

The imperfect subjunctive is formed from the third person plural of the preterite. The **-ron** ending is dropped, and the subjunctive endings (**-ra, -ras, -ra, -´ramos, -rais, -ran**) are added.

Infinitive	Third Person Plural Preterite	First Person Singular Subjunctive
Regular		
cantar	cantaron	cantara
comer	comieron	comiera
escribir	escribieron	escribiera
Stem Changes in Preterite		
dormir	durmieron	durmiera
sentir	sintieron	sintiera
Irregular in Preterite		
ir	fueron	fuera
hacer	hicieron	hiciera
dar	dieron	diera
traer	trajeron	trajera
venir	vinieron	viniera

Note. There is an alternate form of the imperfect subjunctive, not used by all speakers but frequently used in written Spanish. It has the same base as the above form, but the endings are as follows: -se, -ses, -se, -´semos, -seis, -sen. For example, **hablara** would be **hablase**.

Exercise A. Change from the present indicative to the imperfect subjunctive. Use the -ra form.

1. bebo	_____	6. dice	_____
2. recibimos	_____	7. volvemos	_____
3. bailan	_____	8. pones	_____
4. andamos	_____	9. saben	_____
5. vas	_____	10. puedo	_____

USE OF THE IMPERFECT SUBJUNCTIVE

The imperfect subjunctive is parallel to the present subjunctive in usage in noun, adjective, and adverb clauses, except that the point of view is the past.

Present:

Quiero que vayas.   I want you to go.

Past:

Quería que fueras.   I wanted you to go.

Present:

No hay nadie que cante bien.   There is nobody who sings well.

Past:

No había nadie que cantara bien.   There was nobody who sang well.

Present:

No trabajaremos a menos que nos paguen bien.   We won't work unless they pay us well.

Past:

No trabajábamos a menos que nos pagaran bien.   We wouldn't work unless they paid us well.

IF CLAUSES

The present subjunctive may never be used in "if" clauses. In fact, the subjunctive is never used in neutral clauses. Only the indicative is used (present meaning generates present form, and past meaning generates past form).

Si sales a las cinco...   If you leave at 5:00...

Si terminaste primero...   If you finished first...

However, when an unlikely or unreal situation is suggested, Spanish uses the imperfect or past perfect subjunctive. English uses "should" or "were" and the past perfect (or pluperfect). (The past perfect is covered in Chapter 31.)

Si lloveria...   If it should rain...

Si yo fuera él...   If I were he...

Si tuviéramos el dinero...   If we had the money...

Notes.

1. When the imperfect subjunctive follows **si**, the other clause in the sentence generally contains a verb in the conditional:

Si tuviera el dinero,   If I had the money,
iría a Grecia.   I would go to Greece.

Si no estuviera lloviendo, comeríamos afuera.	If it weren't raining, we would eat outside.

2. The imperfect subjunctive is used after **como si** (as if), in contrary-to-fact situations.

Como si fuera experto.	As if he were an expert.
Como si supiera la respuesta.	As if he knew the answer.

Exercise B. Choose the correct answer.

1. Si yo (tenía, tengo, tuviera, tenga) dinero, lo compraré.   _____

2. Si (lloviera, llueve) no voy.   _____

3. Habla como si (esté, está, estaba, estuviera) borracho (drunk).   _____

4. Si él lo hubiera entendido, me lo (habría, había) explicado.   _____

5. Yo no lo (haría, hacía, haré) si fuera Ud.   _____

6. Si yo (fui, soy, sea, fuera) tú, lo escribiría así.   _____

7. Si nosotros (hacemos, hiciéramos, hagamos) un viaje, ¿nos acompañarán Uds.?   _____

8. Si (hubiera, había, tuviera) tenido dinero, habría comprado la casa.   _____

9. Si yo (tendré, tenía, tuviera, tengo) frío, me pongo el abrigo (coat).   _____

10. El maestro habló como si (supo, sabía, supiera) todo.   _____

Exercise C. Write the correct form of the verb.

1. Se despidieron de él como si nunca más (volver) a verlo.   _____

2. Si pudiera el lagarto (lizard) saltar cincuenta pies, (escaparse) del gato.   _____

3. Si María no puede hacerlo, ¿lo (quiere) hacer Ud.?   _____

4. Si ellos no (llegar) pronto, tendremos que salir sin ellos.   _____

5. Mi amigo camina lentamente, como si le (doler) los pies.   _____

6. Si yo tuviera la oportunidad, (pasar) otro año en España.   _____

7. Si no (hacer) buen tiempo, no iríamos.   _____

8. Si Uds. no (vender) muchos lápices, no ganarán mucho dinero.   _____

9. Si nieva, nosotros no (ir).   _____

10. ¿Dónde vivirías si se (vender) tu casa?   _____

11. Mi perro come como si (tener) hambre.   _____

12. Si Juan (poder) hacerlo, le pagaríamos diez   _____
    dólares.

13. La pobre mujer no estaría tan cansada si no   _____
    (tener) tantos hijos.

14. Si yo (estudiar) más, sacaré mejores notas   _____
    (grades).

15. Si Pepe hubiera trabajado todo el verano, él   _____
    (haber) ganado bastante dinero para ir a
    Europa.

PRESENT PERFECT AND PLUPERFECT SUBJUNCTIVES

Spanish has two perfect tenses in the subjunctive. These are used when a subjunctive is needed in the dependent clause.

PRESENT PERFECT   The present perfect subjunctive is formed by using the present subjunctive of **haber** followed by a past participle. It corresponds to the auxiliary verb "has" plus past participle in English.

Present Subjunctive of Haber Plus Past Participle

haya	hayamos	
hayas	hayáis	+ past participle
haya	hayan	

Examples.

Espero que hayas entendido.	I hope you have understood.
but: Han entendido. (Indicative)	They have understood.
Me alegro de que hayan venido.	I'm glad they have come.
but: Han venido.	They have come.

PLUPERFECT SUBJUNCTIVE   The pluperfect subjunctive is formed by using the imperfect subjunctive of **haber** followed by the past participle. This corresponds to "had" plus past participle in English (again, in structures that require the subjunctive).

Imperfect Subjunctive of Haber Plus Past Participle

hubiera	hubiéramos	
hubieras	hubiérais	+ past participle
hubiera	hubieran	

Examples.

Si ellos hubieran llamado, habríamos esperado.	If they had called, we would have waited.
But: Habían llamado. (Indicative)	They had called.
Dudábamos que hubieran estado allí.	We doubted that they had been there.
But: Habían estado allí. (Indicative)	They had been there.

Note. The present perfect subjunctive is used when the verb in the main clause is expressed in the present or future and the verb in the dependent clause refers to a past action. The pluperfect subjunctive is used in the dependent clause when the main verb is in a past tense or in the conditional, in the case of an "if" clause.

Exercise A. Fill in the blank with the correct form of the present subjunctive or the pluperfect subjunctive, whichever is required.

1. Es posible que Juan ya _____ salido.
2. Ellos se alegraban de que no _____ llovido.
3. Dudo que el correo (mail) _____ llegado.
4. Espero que mi novio me _____ escrito una carta.
5. Si Paco _____ entendido, me lo habría explicado.
6. Yo no creía que ellos _____ dicho eso.
7. El empleado no quería terminar el proyecto hasta que su jefe (boss) le _____ explicado los detalles.
8. Yo habría pasado todo el año en Italia si _____ tenido la oportunidad.
9. Prefiero esperar hasta que ellos _____ arreglado (fixed) mi coche.
10. Es lástima que ella no _____ podido visitar a su amigo.

SECTION I   **A. Give the present subjunctive.**

1. poner: tú   _____
2. volver: nosotros   _____
3. ver: ellos   _____
4. saber: él   _____
5. buscar: usted   _____
6. ir: yo   _____
7. dar: vosotros   _____
8. conocer: ustedes   _____
9. oír: tú   _____
10. dormir: yo   _____

B. Change to the command form.

1. tú lees   _____
2. usted habla   _____
3. ustedes comen   _____
4. tú haces   _____
5. vosotros miráis   _____

C. Translate.

1. What do you (usted) want me to do?   _____
2. I wouldn't do that if I were you.   _____
3. If she had known, she would have gone. _____
4. They doubt that it is there.   _____
5. I hope that it rains.   _____

SECTION II   **A. Fill in the blank with the appropriate form of the verb.**

1. Quiero que ustedes (volver) _____.
2. Juan esperaba que ella (escribir) _____.

3. Si yo tuviera el tiempo, (ir) _____ a San Francisco.

4. Ella prefiere que nosotros (venir) _____ temprano.

5. Ellos saben que Eduardo (estar) _____ enfermo.

6. Dudo que Paco lo (haber) _____ terminado.

7. El profesor espera que nosotros lo (preparar) _____.

8. No es necesario que ustedes (quedarse) _____.

9. Ellos habrían comprado el coche si (haber) _____ tenido el dinero.

10. Nosotros iremos ahora si (poder) _____.

B. Rewrite in the future.

1. vamos   _____

2. hemos comprado   _____

3. llegan   _____

4. está viajando   _____

5. comes   _____

6. dice   _____

7. hago   _____

8. termináis   _____

9. han hecho   _____

10. buscas   _____

C. Translate.

1. Did you (tú) say you hope to buy the house?

   _____

2. No, I said I hope my brother buys it.

   _____

3. It's impossible for us to do it today.

   _____

4. What do you (ustedes) want him to do?

   _____

5. When I go to New York, I will visit the museums.

   _____

ANSWERS

CHAPTER 2

Exercise A

1. las madres
2. las ciudades
3. las escuelas
4. las facultades
5. las montañas
6. las familias

Exercise B

1. los chicos
2. los coches
3. los relojes
4. los doctores
5. los pasos

Exercise C

1. hermanito
2. platito
3. muchachita
4. cochecito
5. gatita

Exercise D

Across

1. tío
2. hermano
4. cocina
5. chica
6. gato
8. comida
11. nombre
12. perro

Down

1. tocadiscos
2. libro
5. cuadro
7. árbol
9. mano
10. ancla

CHAPTER 3

Exercise A

1. el padre de Carmen
2. el coche de Ricardo
3. la hermana de Anita
4. el gato de la hermana
5. el perro de la muchacha

Exercise B

1. de las montañas
2. del hombre
3. al coche
4. de los libros
5. a la ciudad

CHAPTER 4

Exercise A

1. Dónde
2. Quién
3. Qué
4. Cómo
5. Para qué
6. Por qué
7. Cuánto
8. Cuántos
9. Cuál
10. Cuándo

CHAPTER 5

Exercise A

1. rojas, amarillas
2. pequeña
3. moderna
4. largas
5. extranjeros
6. delgados
7. bonitas
8. nerviosos
9. caro
10. cómodas

Exercise B

1. unas lecciones fáciles
   some easy lessons
2. dos corbatas grises
   two gray ties
3. una mujer fuerte
   a strong woman
4. los examenes difíciles
   the difficult exams
5. los chicos pobres
   the poor boys

Exercise C

1. los bailes nacionales
2. las niñas felices
3. los chicos jóvenes
4. los profesores impresionantes
5. las plumas azules

Exercise D

1. Los actores son franceses.
2. Los sombreros son españoles.
3. Juan es alemán.
4. Los hombres son ingleses.
5. Mi abuela es irlandesa.

Exercise E.

1. italiana
2. mexicanas
3. peruana
4. alemanes
5. holandesa

Exercise F

1. demasiados
2. bastante
3. tanto
4. tantas
5. poco
6. pocos

Exercise G

1. su
2. tu

3. mi
4. sus
5. su
6. su
7. vuestra
8. nuestros
9. tus
10. sus

Exercise H

1. su familia
2. nuestra escuela
3. mis amigos
4. su padre
5. sus fotos

Exercise I

Across

1. amarillo
3. rico
5. guapo
7. fácil
8. frío
9. azul
11. enfermo
12. pobre

Down

2. limpio
3. rojo
4. dificil
6. cansado
8. fuerte
10. triste

CHAPTER 6

Exercise A

1. lavas
2. ayudan
3. llamo
4. compráis
5. invitamos
6. preguntan
7. regresas
8. baila
9. enseña
10. regreso

Exercise B

1. estudian (g)
2. prepara (d)
3. necesito (b)
4. bailamos (c)
5. cantan (f)
6. gana (e)
7. miramos (j)
8. compra (i)
9. viajan (h)
10. mandamos (a)

Exercise C

1. mandas
2. cambio

3. trabaja
4. escuchan
5. gana
6. viajan
7. regresamos
8. pasas
9. compra
10. bailamos

Exercise D

1. Sí, miro el programa.
2. No, no enseñamos la geografía.
3. Sí, deseamos más cáfe.
4. No, no compro muchos discos.
5. Sí, preparamos la comida.
6. Sí, canto bien.
7. Sí, regresamos mañana.
8. No, no viajo en octubre.
9. Sí, dejamos una propina.
10. Sí, necesitamos agua.

Exercise E

1. Están en casa de Julia.
2. Julia contesta la puerta.
3. Ocho jóvenes escuchan discos.
4. Toman refrescos.
5. José trabaja en una zapatería.
6. Estudia mucho.
7. Estudia química, biología, historia, matemáticas aplicadas, y francés.
8. Habla francés un poco.

Exercise F

1. Ayudo a mi padre.
2. Invitan a David.
3. Visitamos a Beatríz.
4. (Él) enseña a Pedro.
5. (Ella) pregunta a Juan.

Exercise G

1. respondes
2. corre
3. aprende
4. venden
5. leemos
6. bebéis
7. come
8. prometes
9. vendo
10. rompe

Exercise H

1. debe
2. bebe
3. esconde
4. corre
5. comprende
6. vende
7. coméis
8. ponemos
9. leen
10. promete

Exercise I

1. Sí, leo mucho. Yes, I read a lot.
2. Como _____ en el restaurante. I eat _____ in the restaurant.
3. Sí, comprendemos el español. Yes, we understand Spanish.
4. Sí, respondemos en español. Yes, we answer in Spanish.
5. Sí, corro diariamente. Yes, I run daily.
6. Sí, rompo muchas cosas. Yes, I break a lot of things.
7. Sí, vendemos la casa. Yes, we sell (are selling) the house.
8. Sí, debo dinero a mi padre. Yes, I owe my father money.

Exercise J

1. escribe
2. abre
3. subimos
4. asistes
5. deciden

Exercise K

1. escribe
2. recibo
3. asistís
4. admites
5. abren
6. decidimos
7. vive
8. sube

Exercise L

1. Sí, abro el libro en la clase. Yes, I open the book in class.
2. Asisto a _____. I attend _____.
3. Sí, vivo cerca de la escuela. Yes, I live near school.
4. Escribo _____. I write _____.
5. Sí, admito mis errores. Yes, I admit my errors.
6. Sí, recibo muchas cartas. Yes, I receive many letters.

Exercise M

1. Marta y Mario hablan en la cocina.
2. Las llaves de Mario están en la mesa.
3. El padre necesita regresar a la oficina.
4. Ellos corren en la playa.
5. Marta lee un artículo sobre las Naciones Unidas.

CHAPTER 7

Exercise A

1. está
2. están

3. estás
4. está
5. está
6. estoy
7. están
8. estamos
9. está
10. están

Exercise B

1. es
2. eres
3. son
4. soy
5. es
6. es
7. es
8. son
9. somos
10. es

Exercise C

1. Sí, estoy en casa en este momento.
2. Sí, soy simpático.
3. Sí, somos estudiantes excelentes.
4. Sí, soy una persona nerviosa.
5. Sí, estoy nervioso en este momento.
6. Sí, soy joven.
7. Sí, estoy contento.
8. Sí, ellas están cansadas.
9. Sí, el señor Rubio es rico.
10. Sí, Carolina es bonita.

Exercise D

1. es
2. están
3. soy
4. estoy
5. somos
6. está
7. es
8. es
9. es
10. es

Exercise E

1. Somos de California.
2. (Ellos) están muy ocupados.
3. ¿Estás enfermo hoy?
4. ¿Dónde está Carlos?
5. El es mi amigo.
6. Ella está bonita.
7. El es muy listo.
8. Mañana es viernes.
9. Es importante.
10. La casa es moderna.

Exercise F

1. Es
2. Hay
3. Son
4. Esfan
5. Hay

6. Están
7. Hay
8. Son, son
9. Es
10. Hay

CHAPTER 8

Exercise A

1. uno; once; ciento
2. dos; doce; veinte; doscientos
3. tres; trece; treinta; trescientos
4. cuatro; catorce; cuarenta; cuatrocientos
5. cinco; quince; cincuenta; quinientos
6. seis; dieciséis; sesenta; seiscientos
7. siete; diecisiete; setenta; setecientos
8. ocho; dieciocho; ochenta; ochocientos
9. nueve; diecinueve; noventa; novecientos
10. cincuenta y dos; sesenta y siete; setenta y cinco; ochenta y seis.

Exercise B

1. décimo
2. tercera
3. primero
4. quinta
5. Segundo
6. primer
7. octavo

Exercise C

1. Hoy es jueves el diez de agosto.
2. Mañana es miércoles el cinco de enero.
3. Mi cumpleaños es el tres de junio.
4. Si hoy es lunes, mañana es martes.
5. Si hoy es viernes, mañana es sábado.

Exercise D

1. Hoy es _____.
2. Es el _____ de _____.
3. La primavera empieza el veintiuno de marzo.
4. El invierno empieza el veintiuno de diciembre.
5. El año escolar empieza en septiembre.

Exercise E

1. Son las dos y cuarto (y quince).
2. Son las diez y veinticinco.
3. Es la una y diez.
4. A mediodía.
5. Son las seis de la mañana.
6. Son las cuatro y cuarenta (las cinco menos veinte) de la tarde.
7. A las ocho y media (y treinta) de la tarde.

8. Son las tres cuarenta y cinco (las cuatro menos cuarto).

CHAPTER 9

Exercise A

1. almuerzas
2. devuelve
3. vuelve
4. podemos
5. suena
6. recuerdo
7. vuela
8. envolvéis
9. llueve
10. cuentan

Exercise B

1. Una docena de huevos cuesta _____. A dozen eggs costs _____.
2. Generalmente almuerzan en _____. They generally eat in _____.
3. Los pájaros vuelan al sur en el invierno. Birds fly south in the winter.
4. Sí, podemos trabajar mañana. Yes, we can work tomorrow.
5. Sí, llueve mucho en la ciudad donde vivo. Yes, it rains a lot in the city where I live.
6. Si, recuerdo la canción. Yes, I remember the song.
7. Vuelvo a casa a las _____. I return home at _____.
8. Sí, juego al tenis. Yes, I play tennis.

Exercise C

1. puedo
2. huelen
3. envuelve
4. recordamos
5. pruebas
6. cuenta
7. jugáis
8. encuentro

Exercise D

1. nieva
2. cierra
3. quieren
4. comenzamos
5. quiebra
6. entiendes
7. pierde
8. despierta
9. empezáis
10. piensa

Exercise E

1. calienta
2. defienden

3. tiembla
4. gobierna
5. comienza, empieza
6. encendemos
7. nieva
8. queréis

Exercise F

1. prefiero
2. duermes
3. miente
4. sugiere
5. mueren

Exercise G

1. duermo
2. prefiere
3. sugiere
4. mienten
5. mueren

Exercise H

1. fríe
2. eligen
3. despide
4. reímos
5. pido
6. repetís
7. vistes
8. corrige

CHAPTER 10

Exercise A

1. Van a la playa.
2. Estoy bien, gracias.
3. Damos el libro a Pedro.
4. Vamos al cine.
5. ¿Cuándo van a volver?
6. ¿Doy el dinero al cajero?
7. Voy a empezar mañana.

Exercise B

1. Vengo a la escuela a las _____.
   I come to school at _____.
2. Pongo mi tarea en _____. I put
   my homework on _____.
3. Sí, hago todos los ejercicios. Yes, I
   do all the exercises.
4. Sí, digo la verdad a mi profesora.
   Yes, I tell the truth to my teacher.
5. Sí, oigo la música. Yes, I hear the
   music.
6. Salgo _____ (mañana, el
   viernes, etc.) para México. I leave
   _____ (tomorrow, Friday, etc.)
   for Mexico.
7. Traigo _____ (mi libro, mi
   pluma) a la clase. I bring
   _____ (my book, my pen, etc.)
   to class.

8. No, no caigo mucho. No, I don't
   fall much.
9. Mi bicicleta vale ciento ochenta
   dólares. My bicycle is worth one
   hundred and eighty dollars.
10. Sí, tengo una favorita camisa vieja.
    Yes, I have a favorite old shirt.

Exercise C

1. reconozco
2. traducimos
3. conduce
4. parece
5. obedecen
6. ofrezco
7. conocen
8. aparece

Exercise D

1. ¿Ves mi pluma?
2. No sé la fecha.
3. Vemos a nuestros amigos los
   sábados.
4. Ella no sabe mi nombre.
5. Veo unos árboles bonitos.

Exercise E

1. sé
2. conocemos
3. sabe
4. conocen; saben
5. sabemos
6. conozco
7. saben
8. conoces

Exercise F

1. ¿Tiene Ud. hambre?
2. Mi amigo tiene quince años.
3. Tenemos mucha sed.
4. El no tiene razón todo el tiempo.
5. Ella siempre tiene prisa.
6. No tengo miedo.
7. ¿Qué tienen ellos?

Exercise G

1. hace calor
2. Hace mucho frío.
3. hace buen tiempo
4. hace viento
5. Hace sol
6. No hace fresco

Exercise H

1. tengo
2. están
3. es
4. hace, hace
5. tiene
6. tiene
7. está
8. tiene
9. estoy
10. son

Exercise I

1. Tenemos frío.
2. El tiene prisa.
3. Tienen miedo a los gatos.
4. ¿Tiene Ud. mucha hambre?
5. Tengo suerte.
6. ¿Quién tiene sed?

CHAPTER 11

Exercise A

1. esperando
2. leyendo
3. durmiendo
4. trayendo
5. hablando
6. estudiando
7. vendiendo
8. tocando
9. sirviendo
10. diciendo

Exercise B

1. Están viajando por los Estados
   Unidos.
2. ¿Estás escribiendo la carta?
3. El niño está corriendo por la calle.
4. Estamos abriendo las ventanas.
5. Estoy cantando en español.
6. ¿Quién está explicando la lección?
7. Están haciendo la tarea en casa.
8. ¿Estáis trabajando en el jardín?

Exercise C

1. están jugando
2. está enseñando
3. No está lloviendo
4. están haciendo
5. están describiendo
6. Sigues (continúas) escribiendo
7. está perdiendo
8. estoy comiendo

CHAPTER 12

Exercise A

1. Las comprendemos
2. Lo miran.
3. Lo espero.
4. Los compramos.
5. ¿Quién las vende?

Exercise B

1. Sí, los oímos.
2. No, no los vemos.
3. Sí, la tengo.
4. Sí, las visito.
5. Sí, las aprendo.

Exercise C

1. They know me.
2. Do they listen to you?
3. She is looking (looks) for you
   (pl.).

4. He waits for us.
5. I cannot hear you.

Exercise D

1. Juan Martinez les da dinero.
2. Paquito no nos dice la verdad.
3. Le mando el paquete.
4. Le das una pluma.
5. Les quiero escribir (Quiero escribirles.)

Exercise E

1. El me trae un vaso de agua.
2. Ella nos explica la lección.
3. Juan nos sirve café.
4. Les decimos la hora.
5. ¿Puedes darles la carta? (O: le puedes dar...)

Exercise F

1. Le damos el libro a Mario.
   Se lo damos.
2. Ellos me mandan la invitación.
   Me la mandan.
3. Ella nos trae la comida.
   Nos la trae.
4. Le enseño la lección.
   Se la enseño.
5. El le promete un viaje a Bermuda.
   Se lo promete.

Exercise G

1. el cual
2. lo que
3. lo que
4. que
5. quien
6. que
7. cuyos
8. lo que

CHAPTER 13

Exercise A

1. se duerme
2. te llamas
3. se despiertan
4. me acuesto
5. se divierten
6. nos vamos
7. se entera
8. te enfadas
9. me equivoco
10. os quedáis

Exercise B

1. se asusta
2. nos paseamos
3. se marcha
4. os desayunáis
5. se quita

CHAPTER 14

Exercise A

1. pagaron
2. llevó
3. trabajó
4. escuchaste
5. dejamos
6. regresasteis
7. ganaron
8. compró
9. miramos
10. invitaste
11. almorcé
12. expliqué

Exercise B

1. bailaste
2. llegó
3. pasó
4. regresaron
5. ganamos
6. contaron
7. hablasteis
8. necesitamos
9. compraste
10. pregunté

Exercise C

1. Encontraron a Jaime en la biblioteca.
2. ¿Probaste el guacamole? Es delicioso.
3. Viajé por México el verano pasado.
4. Recordó las palabras y terminó la traducción.
5. ¿Qué soñaste anoche?
6. Mariana estudió el español hace tres años.
7. Almorzamos en casa de Brian el domingo pasado.
8. ¿Ayudaste a Melissa con su tarea?
9. ¿Dónde pasaron el fin de semana?
10. Tomamos café con ella y hablamos de la Argentina.

Exercise D

1. corrí
2. escondió
3. comprendimos
4. prometieron
5. rompiste
6. metió
7. comió
8. perdí
9. encendiste
10. entendimos

Exercise E

1. Sí, comprendimos la pregunta. Yes, we understood the question.
2. Sí, corrí por el parque. Yes, I ran through the park.
3. Sí, asistí a la escuela. Yes, I attended school.
4. Sí, prometí ir con él. Yes, I promised to go with him.
5. No, no rompí el disco. No, I didn't break the record.
6. No, no viví en Chile. No, I didn't live in Chile.
7. Sí, comí mucho. Yes, I ate a lot.
8. Sí, recibí un regalo de mi tía favorita. Yes, I received a gift from my favorite aunt.
9. Sí, les escribimos.
   Yes, we wrote to them.
10. Sí, subieron la montaña.
    Yes, they climbed the mountain.
11. Sí, sufrí mucho cuando aprendí los verbos. I suffered a lot when I learned the verbs.

Exercise F

1. Josefina visitó a su amiga Clara.
2. Tomaron café y galletas en la sala.
3. Beatríz está en Grecia.
4. Escribió que vió los museos de París, comió bien y compró muchas cosas.
5. Regresa en dos semanas.

CHAPTER 15

Exercise A

1. fui
2. fueron
3. fue
4. dimos
5. fue
6. di

Exercise B

1. fui
2. fue
3. fuimos
4. di
5. dimos

Exercise C

1. trajo
2. supe
3. pusiste
4. tuvimos
5. estuvieron
6. pudiste
7. dijeron
8. anduvo
9. cupieron
10. hiciste

Exercise D

1. pudo
2. condujo
3. dijo
4. traduje
5. vinimos
6. estuvisteis
7. detuvo
8. hizo
9. traje
10. pusimos

Exercise E

1. vinimos
2. estuve
3. traduje
4. condujimos
5. tuve

Exercise F

1. no trajimos
2. pude
3. hizo
4. dijo
5. cupieron
6. vino
7. estuvimos
8. puse

Exercise G

1. leyeron
2. oí
3. destruyó
4. creyó
5. cayeron

Exercise H

1. oímos
2. leí
3. caí
4. creímos
5. contribuí

Exercise I

1. no mintió
2. sugirió
3. durmieron
4. sintió
5. preferimos
6. murió

Exercise J

1. corregí
2. pidió
3. sirvió
4. midió
5. frió
6. repetiste
7. sonrió
8. despidieron

Exercise K

1. seguiste
2. reñí

3. sonrieron
4. corrigió
5. serviste

Exercise L

1. anduve
2. trajo
3. leyeron
4. no dijo
5. fuimos
6. conduje
7. repitió
8. dieron
9. fuiste
10. creyó

CHAPTER 16

Exercise A

1. Trabajábamos
2. cenaban
3. daba
4. gastaba
5. estabais
6. nadábamos
7. almorzaban
8. buscaba
9. viajaba
10. pensaba

Exercise B

1. quería
2. devolvía
3. podían
4. sabía
5. hacíamos
6. decía
7. contribuía
8. oías
9. salía
10. pedía

Exercise C

1. era
2. íbamos
3. veíamos
4. iba, visitaba
5. eras

Exercise D

1. tenían
2. sabía
3. recibíamos
4. se acostaban
5. compraba
6. jugaban
7. preparaba
8. íbamos
9. veía
10. eran

CHAPTER 17

Exercise A

1. eran
2. salió
3. comimos
4. volvieron
5. recibimos
6. visitaste
7. hablaba, entró
8. me levantaba
9. veía
10. fue
11. era
12. tenía, vendió

Exercise B

1. salí
2. era
3. eran, tenían
4. iba
5. hacías
6. había
7. pudo, tenía
8. tenía, nací
9. conocí
10. bailó

Exercise C

1. Andrés vivía en Madrid.
2. El Retiro es un parque bonito en Madrid.
3. Andrés iba con su familia o con sus amigos al Retiro.
4. Andrés fue a Barcelona.
5. Vivían en Barcelona.
6. Se llama Tossa de Mar.
7. Es la lengua que se habla en Cataluña.

CHAPTER 18

Exercise A

1. esperan   (b)
2. estudia   (a)
3. trabaja   (e)
4. estamos   (c)
5. estás   (d)

Exercise B

1. Hacía una hora que escuchaban el disco.
2. ¿Cuánto tiempo hacía que estaban allí?
3. Hacía dos días que estaba enfermo.
4. Hacía una hora que hablábamos.
5. Hacía quince minutos que Elsa leía.

Exercise C

1. Vinieron hace dos horas.
2. ¿Cuánto tiempo hace que comiste?
3. Visité Nueva York hace dos años.
4. Vimos al señor Robles hace tres días.
5. ¿Cuánto tiempo hace que ella trabajo allí?

Exercise D

1. Fuimos a España hace dos años.
2. Hace una hora que mi hermana duerme.
3. Hacía treinta minutos que corrían.
4. ¿Cuánto tiempo hace que lees?
5. Hace mucho (tiempo) que llueve.
6. ¿Cuánto tiempo hacía que estaban allí?

CHAPTER 19

Exercise A

1. gusta
2. gusta
3. gusta
4. gusta
5. gustan
6. gustan

Exercise B

1. nos gustó
2. les gusta
3. te gustan
4. no me gustó
5. no le gustaron
6. les gustó

Exercise C

1. a él
2. a nosotros
3. a ti
4. a mí
5. a ella

Exercise D

1. me hace falta
2. nos encanta
3. no te queda
4. le parece (a ella)
5. nos interesan
6. nos sorprendió
7. pasó a ellos

CHAPTER 20

Exercise A

1. No puedo ir tampoco.
2. No hay nada en la mesa.
3. Marisa no tiene ningunos juguetes.
4. No vieron a nadie.
5. No voy ni a la biblioteca ni al museo.
6. Nunca vamos al cine.

Exercise B

1. algo
2. tampoco
3. ya no
4. ni . . . ni
5. nadie
6. alguien
7. ningún
8. algún
9. nadie

Exercise C

1. Nunca leo novelas románticas.
2. No, no invité a nadie al baile.
3. No, no escribí nada en el cuaderno.
4. No viajo ni a España ni a México.
5. No vamos a estudiar tampoco.

Exercise D

1. No hablamos portugués tampoco.
2. No vio a nadie.
3. No trajo nada a la fiesta.
4. Nunca estudian en agosto.
5. ¿Hay alguien en la cocina?

REVIEW TEST 1

Section I

A.

1. está
2. somos
3. es
4. está
5. está
6. es
7. está
8. es
9. son
10. es

B.

1. Usted la escribe a María.
2. Carlos les manda el dinero.
3. Yo le hablo.
4. Yo la veo.
5. Lo quiero mandar. (*or* Quiero mandarlo.)

C.

1. Le gustan.
2. ¿Te gusta mi perro?
3. No nos gustaron esos (OR aquellos) edificios.
4. Les gusta comer enchiladas.
5. Me gusta la hermana de Juan.

Section II

A.

1. traigo
2. comienzas

3. se despiertan
4. quiere
5. digo
6. miramos
7. oye
8. escucháis
9. comemos
10. hago

B.

1. llovió
2. entendí
3. comprendiste
4. cerraron
5. vendimos
6. recordaron
7. volvisteis
8. perdiste
9. abrió
10. hablaron

C.

1. What were you doing when I called?
2. Did you know he arrived this morning?
3. We were going to leave early but we had too much work.
4. What was she saying? I didn't hear.
5. She got up late because she was tired.

CHAPTER 21

Exercise A

1. este
2. aquella
3. esas
4. estas
5. aquel
6. ese
7. estos
8. aquellos
9. Ese
10. Estas

Exercise B

1. tercer
2. primer
3. San; San
4. gran
5. buen
6. mal
7. ningún

Exercise C

1. Jaime es más alto que su padre.
2. Tengo más discos que Teodoro.
3. El gato no es tan grande como el perro.
4. Estoy tan ocupado como el señor Romero.

5. Ellos compran tantas flores como Ana.
6. El café es mejor que el té.
7. Las hamburguesas en la cafeteriá son malas, pero las enchiladas son peores.

Exercise D

1. Lo interesante
2. rubia
3. la pequeña
4. Los ricos
5. El alto

Exercise E

1. abiertas
2. hecha
3. conocido
4. preparada
5. escritas
6. cerrado

Exercise F

1. fácilmente, easily
2. lentamente, slowly
3. probablemente, probably
4. rápidamente, quickly
5. alegremente, happily
6. claramente, clearly
7. realmente, in reality, truly
8. necesariamente, necessarily
9. completamente, completely
10. posiblemente, possibly

Exercise G

1. diligentemente
2. correctamente
3. generalmente
4. inmediatamente
5. finalmente
6. fácilmente
7. perfectamente
8. frecuentemente

CHAPTER 22

Exercise A

1. tengo   tenga   tengan
2. cierro   cierre   cierren
3. vuelvo   vuelva   vuelvan
4. oigo   oiga   oigan
5. aprendo   aprenda   aprendan
6. vengo   venga   vengan
7. pongo   ponga   pongan
8. leo   lea   lean
9. duermo   duerma   duerman
10. repito   repita   repitan

Exercise B

1. abra
2. traduzcan
3. piense
4. escriban
5. mande

6. traigan
7. sea
8. conduzca
9. vayan
10. dé

Exercise C

1. Sí, sírvala. No, no la sirva.
2. Sí, hágalos. No, no los haga.
3. Sí, ciérrela. No, no la cierre.
4. Sí, cómalo. No, no lo coma.
5. Sí, désela. No, no se la dé.

Exercise D

1. Sí, búsquenlo, No, no lo busquen.
2. Sí, cómprenlo. No, no lo compren.
3. Sí, cómanlo. No, no lo coman.
4. Sí, límpienla. No, no la limpien.
5. Sí, cocínenlas. No, no las cocinen.

CHAPTER 23

Exercise A

1. estará
2. volverán
3. irán
4. llegará
5. terminaré
6. te vestirás
7. veremos
8. cenaréis

Exercise B

1. escribiré
2. venderemos
3. terminarás
4. descansaré
5. vivirán

Exercise C

1. tendremos
2. podrá
3. valdrán
4. saldrá
5. vendrás
6. sabré
7. pondrán
8. cabremos
9. dirá
10. querrán

Exercise D

1. correrías
2. buscarían
3. traduciriá
4. volveríamos
5. ayudaría
6. irías
7. escogería
8. visitaría

Exercise E

1. querría
2. cabrían

3. haría
4. vendríamos
5. valdría
6. podría
7. tendrían
8. saldríais
9. pondría
10. dirías

Exercise F

1. escribiré, escribiría
2. repetirá, repetiría
3. harás, harías
4. se acostará, se acostaría
5. tendrán, tendrían
6. habrá, habría
7. podré, podría
8. sabremos, sabríamos
9. dirás, dirías
10. venderá, vendería

Exercise G

1. dormiremos
2. prepararía
3. serán
4. habrá
5. me gustaría
6. estaría
7. tendrá
8. saldrían
9. no manejaré, conduciré
10. Haría

CHAPTER 24

Exercise A

1. da
2. no vuelvas
3. comed
4. no habléis
5. haz
6. no leas
7. sal
8. estudiad
9. no cantes
10. pon

Exercise B

1. salid
2. tráelo
3. bailéis
4. ven
5. no lo hagas
6. escribidlas
7. dila
8. no lo comas

CHAPTER 25

Exercise A

1. de
2. a
3. de
4. de

5. de
6. a
7. de
8. a
9. a
10. a

Exercise B

1. Before leaving, Vicente paid the bill.
2. We eat in order to live.
3. We're going to go to the beach after having supper.

CHAPTER 26

Exercise A

1. por
2. por
3. para
4. por
5. para
6. por
7. para
8. por
9. por
10. por
11. para
12. por
13. para
14. para
15. para
16. por
17. por
18. por
19. por
20. por

Exercise B

1. por
2. para
3. para
4. para
5. para
6. para
7. por
8. por
9. por
10. por

Exercise C

1. pero
2. sino
3. sino
4. pero
5. pero
6. sino
7. sino
8. pero
9. sino
10. sino

CHAPTER 27

Exercise A

1. bebido
2. cantado
3. recibido
4. llegado
5. subido
6. almorzado
7. aprendido
8. sufrido
9. perdido
10. pedido

Exercise B

1. ha comido
2. han trabajado
3. Has abierto
4. he leído
5. hemos roto
6. habéis estado
7. han salido
8. ha dicho

Exercise C

1. se habían levantado
2. habíamos escrito
3. habían vendido
4. había muerto
5. había oído
6. habíais hecho
7. habían descubierto
8. habías puesto

Exercise D

1. he estado trabajando
2. hemos estado visitando
3. he estado leyendo
4. había estado viviendo
5. hemos estado diciendo

Exercise E

1. Alberto no ha estudiado.
2. Fernando ya sabe todo.
3. Alberto llevó a su perro al médico.
4. El perro estaba enfermo.
5. Quiere comer.

Exercise F

1. habré vivido
2. habrá terminado
3. habrán visto
4. habremos visitado
5. habrás vuelto
6. habréis decidido
7. habrás traído
8. habrán insistido

Exercise G

1. habríais ido
2. habrías hecho
3. habría creído
4. habrían podido
5. habría dado

6. habría dicho
7. nos habríamos acostado
8. habrían bebido

Exercise H

1. había dicho
2. él ha roto
3. ellos han abierto
4. había empezado
5. habré vuelto
6. habríamos tenido
7. he estado
8. habrán hecho
9. habría pedido
10. no se han vestido

CHAPTER 28

Exercise A

1. La comida fue preparada por la criada.
2. Esos cuadros magníficos fueron pintados por Picasso.
3. Concha es amada de Julio.
4. Las cuentas serán pagadas por el Sr. Rodriguez.
5. La profesora es respetada de sus alumnos.

Exercise B

1. fue descubierta por
2. es respetado de
3. fueron corregidos por
4. será servida por
5. fue destruida por

Exercise C

1. Se preparan los mariscos.
2. Se sirvió la comida a las nueve.
3. Se usó madera para construir la casa.
4. Se habla francés en el Canadá.
5. No se sabe nada de su vida.
6. Se vendieron las chaquetas a un precio bajo.
7. Anoche se celebró su cumpleaños.
8. El año que viene se producirá más café.

Exercise D

1. se abren
2. No se fuma mucho
3. se hablan
4. se dice
5. se venden
6. Se cree
7. se construyeron
8. se puede ver
9. Se dice
10. se oyen

CHAPTER 29

Exercise A

1. traigamos
2. hablen
3. tengas
4. salgan
5. espere
6. haga
7. entienda
8. pierda

Exercise B

1. Dudo que estén aquí.
2. ¿Quiere Ud. que él salga?
3. Es imposible que estudiemos hoy.
4. Es lástima que ella no pueda venir.
5. Prefiero ir temprano.
6. Ella está contenta (feliz) de que haga sol.
7. ¿Qué quiere ella que yo diga?

Exercise C

1. hable
2. entiende
3. sepa
4. crea
5. quiere
6. está
7. sepa
8. incluya
9. puede
10. está

Exercise D

1. hable
2. tiene
3. sea
4. tiene
5. juegue
6. gusten
7. está
8. valga
9. viaje
10. dude

Exercise E

1. Ojalá que él haga el trabajo.
2. Ojalá que ellos estén aquí.
3. Ojalá que nosotros tengamos todo.
4. Ojalá que usted salga bien en el examen.
5. Ojalá que ella me diga el secreto.
6. Ojalá que tú traigas los discos.

CHAPTER 30

Exercise A

1. bebiera
2. recibiéramos

3. bailaran
4. anduviéramos
5. fueras
6. dijera
7. volviéramos
8. pusieras
9. supieran
10. pudiéramos

Exercise B

1. tengo
2. llueve
3. estuviera
4. habría
5. haría
6. fuera
7. hacemos
8. hubiera
9. tengo
10. supiera

Exercise C

1. volverían
2. se escaparía
3. quiere
4. llegan
5. dolieran
6. pasaría
7. hiciera
8. venden
9. vamos (o: iremos)
10. vendiera
11. tuviera
12. pudiera
13. tuviera
14. estudió
15. habría

CHAPTER 31

Exercise A

1. haya salido
2. hubiera llovido
3. haya llegado
4. haya escrito
5. hubiera entendido
6. hubieran dicho
7. hubiera explicado
8. hubiera tenido
9. hayan arreglado
10. haya podido

FINAL REVIEW TEST

Section I

A.

1. pongas
2. volvamos
3. vean

4. sepa
5. busque
6. vaya
7. deis
8. conozcan
9. oigas
10. duerma

B.

1. lee
2. hable
3. coman
4. haz
5. mirad

C.

1. ¿Qué quieres que yo haga?
2. Yo no haría eso si fuera usted.
3. Si ella hubiera sabido, habría ido.
4. Dudan que esté allí.
5. Espero que llueva.

Section II

A.

1. vuelvan
2. escribiera
3. iría
4. vengamos
5. está
6. haya
7. preparemos
8. se queden
9. hubieran
10. podemos

B.

1. iremos
2. habremos comprado
3. llegarán
4. estará viajando
5. comerás
6. dirás
7. haré
8. terminaréis
9. habrán hecho
10. buscarás

C.

1. ¿Dijiste que esperas comprar la casa?
2. No, dije que espero que la compre mi hermano.
3. Es imposible que lo hagamos hoy.
4. ¿Qué quieren Uds. que él haga?
5. Cuando yo vaya a Nueva York, visitaré los museos.

WORD LIST

A

abogada, *f.* woman lawyer

abogado, *m.* lawyer

abrelatas, *m.* can opener

abrigo, *m.* overcoat, wrap

abril, *m.* April

abrir, *m.* to open

abuela, *f.* grandmother

abuelo, *m.* grandfather

abuelos, *m., f.* grandparents

acabar, to finish; de + infinitive, to have just + verb (e.g., Acabo de comer; I have just eaten.)

accidente, *m.* accident

acordarse, to remember

acostarse, to go to bed

acostumbrarse, to become accustomed

activo, activa, *a.* active, lively

actor, *m.* actor

actriz, *f.* actress

admitir, to admit, accept, allow

adonde, where

aéreo, aerial; por _____ by airmail

afuera, outside

agente, *m.* agent

agosto, *m.* August

agrio,a, *a.* bitter, sour

agua, *f.* water

águila, *f.* eagle

ahí, there

ahora, now

aire, *m.* air

albóndiga, *f.* meatball

alegrarse, to be glad, rejoice

alemán, alemana, German

algo, something

alguien, someone

algún, alguna(s), alguno(s), some

allá, there

allí, there

almorzar, to have lunch

alquilar, to rent

alrededor, *adv.* around

alumno,a, *m., f.* student

amable, *a.* kind

amarillo,a, *a.* yellow

amigo,a, *m., f.* friend

amor, *m.* love

andar, to walk

anillo, *m.* ring

animal, *m.* animal

año, *m.* year

anoche, *m.* last year

anteayer, *m.* the day before yesterday

anuncio, *m.* announcement

aparecer, to appear

apartamento, *m.* apartment

aplicado,a, *a.* industrious

aprender, to learn

aquel, aquella, *demons. a.* that

aquello, *neuter pron.* that; that thing

aquellos, *demons. a.* those

aquí, here

árabe, Arabic

árbol, *m.* tree

arete, *m.* earring

argentino,a, *a.* Argentinian

arma, *f.* weapon

arquitecto, *m.* architect

arreglado,a, *a.* fixed, arranged

arte, *m.* art

artículo, *m.* article

artista, *m., f.* artist

así, so, like this, in such a way

asistir, to attend

asustarse, to be frightened

atreverse, to dare, venture

atribuir, to attribute

aunque, although

autobús, *m.* bus

autor,a, *m., f.* author

avión, *m.* airplane

avisar, to warn, to let (someone) know

ayer, *m.* yesterday

ayudar, to help

azúcar, *m.* sugar

azul, *a.* blue

B

bailar, to dance

baile, *m.* dance

bajo,a, *a.* low, short

banco, *m.* bank

bandera, *f.* flag

bandido, *m.* bandit

barato,a, *a.* inexpensive

barco, *m.* boat

bastante, *a.* enough; *adv.* enough; rather

basura, *f.* garbage

basurero, *m.* garbage can; garbage collector

beber, to drink

bebé, *m.* baby

béisbol, *m.* baseball

bello,a, *a.* beautiful

biblioteca, *f.* library

bicicleta, *f.* bicycle

bien, *adv.* well
biología, *f.* biology
blanco,a, *a.* white
blusa, *f.* blouse
bonito,a, *a.* pretty
borracho,a, *a.* drunk
botella, *f.* bottle
botellazo, *m.* blow with a bottle
botón, *m.* button
brasileño,a, *a.* Brazilian
bravo,a, *a.* wild, angry
brazo, *m.* arm
buen, bueno,a, *a.* good
buscar, to look for

C

caballo, *m.* horse
caber, to fit
cabeza, *f.* head
cada, each
caer, to fall
café, *m.* coffee
caja, *f.* box
cajón, *m.* drawer
calentar, to heat
caliente, *a.* hot
callarse, to be quiet
calle, *f.* street
calor, *m.* heat
cama, *f.* bed
camarero,a, *m., f.* waiter
cambiar, to change, exchange
caminar, to walk
camisa, *f.* shirt
campana, *f.* bell
campo, *m.* field, country
canción, *f.* song
cansado,a, *a.* tired
cantar, to sing
capítulo, *m.* chapter
caro,a, expensive
carta, *f.* letter
cartera, *f.* wallet; briefcase
casa, *f.* house
casi, almost
caso, *m.* case
catedral, *f.* cathedral
catorce, fourteen
celebrar, to celebrate
cena, *f.* supper
cenar, to have supper
centro, *m.* center; downtown
cepillarse, to brush
cerca, near
cerrado,a, *a.* closed
cerrar, to close
cesta, *f.* basket
chaqueta, *f.* jacket
cheque, *m.* check
chica, *f.* girl
chico, *m.* boy
chileno,a, Chilean
chiste, *m.* joke

cien, ciento, one hundred
cigarro, *m.* cigar
cinco, five
cincuenta, fifty
cine, *m.* movie theater
cinta, *f.* tape
cinturón, *m.* belt
cita, *f.* date, appointment
ciudad, *f.* city
claro,a, *a.* clear
clase, *f.* class
clima, *m.* climate
clínica, *f.* clinic
coche, *m.* car
cocina, *f.* kitchen
cocinar, to cook
cocinero,a, *m., f.* cook
codazo, *m.* blow with the elbow
codo, *m.* elbow
colchón, *m.* mattress
cólera, *f.* anger; *m.* cholera
colombiano,a, *a.* Colombian
comenzar, to begin
comer, to eat
cometa, *f.* kite; *m.* comet
comida, *f.* food
como, like, as
cómo, *adv.* how
cómodo,a, *a.* comfortable
composición, *f.* composition
comprar, to buy
comprender, to understand
concha, *f.* shell
concierto, *m.* concert
conducir, to drive, conduct
conferencia, *f.* lecture; conference
conmigo, with me
conocer, to know, be acquainted
conseguir, to obtain
consentir, to consent; to pamper
consigo, with himself, herself,
    themselves
construir, to build
contaminación, *f.* pollution;
    contamination
contar, to count; to tell
contento,a, *a.* happy
contestar, to answer
contigo, with you
continuar, to continue
contribuir, to contribute
copa, *f.* wine glass
corbata, *f.* necktie
correctamente, correctly
correcto,a, *a.* correct
corregir, to correct
correo, *m.* mail
correr, to run
corrida, *f.* bullfight
corte, *f.* court; *m.* cut
corto,a short
cosa, *f.* thing
costar, to cost
creer, to believe

criada, *f.* maid
cuaderno, *m.* notebook
cuadro, *m.* picture
cual, which
cuando, when
cuanto,a, *a.* how much
cuarenta, forty
cuarto, *m.* fourth; room
cuatro, four
cuatrocientos, four hundred
cubano,a, Cuban
cubierto,a, *a.* covered
cubrir, to cover
cuenta, *f.* account; bill
cueva, *f.* cave
culpar, to blame
cumpleaños, *m.* birthday
cura, *m.* priest; *f.* cure
cuyo,a, whose

D

dar, to give; darse cuenta, to realize
debajo, under
deber, to owe; ought
decidir, to decide
décimo, tenth
decir, to say, tell
dejar, to leave (something behind);
    to allow
delgado,a, *a.* thin
delicioso,a, delicious
demasiado,a *a.* too much
dentista, *m., f.* dentist
dependiente, *m., f.* clerk
deporte, *m.* sport
desaparecer, to disappear
desastre, *m.* disaster
desayunarse, to have breakfast
desayuno, *m.* breakfast
descansar, to rest
descubrir, to discover
desde, since; from
desear, to wish, desire
desierto, *m.* desert
despedir, to fire
despedirse, to say goodbye
despegue, *m.* takeoff
despertador, *m.* alarm clock
despertar, to awaken
despertarse, to wake oneself up
después, after; afterwards
destruir, to destroy
detalle, *m.* detail
devolver, to return (an object)
día, *m.* day
diálogo, *m.* dialogue
diariamente, daily
diccionario, *m.* dictionary
diciembre, December
diecinueve, nineteen
dieciocho, eighteen
dieciséis, sixteen
diecisiete, seventeen

diez,   ten
difícil,   difficult
dinero, *m.*   money
diseñado,a,   designed
disminuir,   to diminish
disolver,   to dissolve
distribuir,   to distribute
divertido,a,   fun, amusing
divertirse,   to have a good time
doce,   twelve
docena, *f.*   dozen
doctor,ra, *m., f.*   doctor
dólar, *m.*   dollar
doler,   to hurt
domingo,   Sunday
donde,   where
dormir,   to sleep
dormirse,   to fall asleep
doscientos,   two hundred
dudable, *a.*   doubtful
dudar,   to doubt
dudoso, *a.*   doubtful
dulce, *a.*   sweet; *noun m.*   candy
durante,   during
duro,a, *a.*   hard

E

económico,a, *a.*   economical
edad, *f.*   age
edificio, *m.*   building
educado,a,   educated
ejercicio, *m.*   exercise
elefante, *m.*   elephant
elegante, *a.*   elegant
elegir,   to elect
ella,   she
ellos,as,   they
empezar,   to begin
empleado,a, *m., f.*   employee
enamorado,a, *a.*   in love
encaje, *m.*   lace
encantador,ra, *a.*   charming,
   enchanting
encantar,   to charm, delight
encender,   to light
encontrar,   to find
enero,   January
enfadarse,   to get angry
enfermo,a, *a.*   sick
enganche, *m.*   hook, trap
engordar,   to fatten
enojar,   to anger
enojarse,   to get angry
enseñar,   to teach
entender,   to understand
enterarse,   to find out
entonces,   then
entrar,   to enter
entre,   between
envolver,   to wrap
envuelto,a,   wrapped
equipo, *m.*   team; equipment
equivocarse,   to be mistaken

error, *m.*   error
esa, *demons. a.*   that
esas,   those
escaparse,   to escape
escoger,   to choose
escolar, *a.*   school
esconder,   to hide
escribir,   to write
escrito,a, *a.*   written
escritor,ra,   writer
escritorio, *m.*   desk
escuchar,   to listen
escuela, *f.*   school
eso,   that
esos,   those
España,   Spain
español, la *a. m., f.*   Spanish
especialidad, *f.*   specialty
esperar,   to hope; to wait; to expect
esposa, *f.*   wife
esposo, *m.*   husband
esquiar,   to ski
esquina, *f.*   corner
estación, *f.*   station; season
estado, *m.*   state
estar,   to be
este, *demons. a.*   this
esto, *demons. pron.*   this
estos, *demons. a.*   these
estudiante, *m., f.*   student
estudiar,   to study
Europa,   Europe
evidente,   evident
examen, *m.*   exam
excelente, *a.*   excellent
experto,a, *m., f.*   expert
explicar,   to explain
extranjero,a, *m., f.*   foreigner

F

fácil, *a.*   easy
facultad, *f.*   faculty
falta, *f.*   lack
faltar   to lack; miss
familia, *f.*   family
famoso,a,   famous
favorito,a,   favorite
febrero,   February
fecha, *f.*   date
feliz, *a.*   happy
feo,a, *a.*   ugly
fila, *f.*   row
flor, *f.*   flower
fotografía, *f.*   photograph
Francia,   France
frase, *f.*   sentence
frecuencia, *f.*   frequency
frecuentemente,   frequently
freír,   to fry
frente, *f.*   front; forehead
frío,a, *a.*   cold
fruta, *f.*   fruit
fuerte, *a.*   strong

fútbol, *m.*   football

G

galleta, *f.*   cookie
gana, *f.*   desire, wish; tener ganas de
   + inf., to want to + verb, to
   feel like
ganar,   to earn; to win
gastar,   to spend
gato,a, *m., f.*   cat
generalmente,   generally
generoso,a, *a.*   generous
gente, *f.*   people
geografía, *f.*   geography
gerente, *m.*   manager
gimnasta, *m.*   gymnast
gobernar,   to govern
gordo,a, *a.*   fat
gozar,   to enjoy
gracias,   thanks
grande, *a.*   large
Grecia,   Greece
griego,   Greek
gris, *a.*   gray
guante, *m.*   glove
guapo,a,   good looking
guardarropas, *m.*   closet
guatemalteco,   Guatemalan
guerra, *f.*   war
guía, *m., f.*   guide
guitarra, *f.*   guitar
gustar,   to please

H

haber,   to have (auxiliary)
hablar,   to speak, talk
hacer,   to make; to do
hacha, *f.*   ax
hacia,   toward
hambre, *f.*   hunger
hartarse,   to be fed up
hay,   there is; there are (from haber)
hecho,a, *a.*   made, done
helado, *m.*   ice cream
herir,   to wound
hermana, *f.*   sister
hermano, *m.*   brother
hermoso,a,   beautiful
hija, *f.*   daughter
hijo, *m.*   son
historia, *f.*   history
hola,   hello
holandés,sa, *a.*   Dutch
hombre, *m.*   man
hombrón, *m.*   large man
honesto,a, *a.*   honest
hora, *f.*   hour, time
hoy, *m.*   today
hueso, *m.*   bone
huevo, *m.*   egg
huir,   to flee

I

iglesia, *f.* church
impedir, to prevent
importante, *a.* important
imposible, *a.* impossible
impresionante, *a.* impressive
impreso,a, published
imprimir, to publish; print
inglés,sa, English
inmediatamente, immediate
insistir, to insist
inteligente, *a.* intelligent
interesante, *a.* interesting
interesar, to interest
interprete, *m., f.* interpreter
invierno, *m.* winter
invitar, to invite
irlandés,sa, *a.* Irish
irse, to go away
isla, *f.* island
Italia, Italy
italiano,a, Italian

J

jamás, never
japonés,sa, *a.* Japanese
jardín, *m.* garden
jefe, *m.* boss
joven, *a.* young
joya, *f.* jewel
jueves, *m.* Thursday
jugar, to play
jugo, *m.* juice
juguete, *m.* toy
julio, *m.* July
junio, *m.* June
junto,a, *a.* joined; (pl.) together

L

lagarta, *f.* female lizard
lagarto, *m.* lizard
lago, *m.* lake
lámpara, *f.* lamp
lápiz, *m.* pencil
la, *def. art., f.* the
lástima, *f.* pity, shame
lata, *f.* can
lavaplatos, *m.* dishwasher
lavar, to wash
lavarse, to wash onself
lección, *f.* lesson
leche, *f.* milk
lectura, *f.* reading
lejos, far
lengua, *f.* tongue; language
lentamente, slowly
levantar, to lift, raise
levantarse, to get up
leyenda, *f.* legend
librería, *f.* bookstore
libro, *m.* book

licenciado,a, *m., f.* lawyer; licensed
límite, *m.* limit
limón, *m.* lemon
limpiar, to clean
limpieza, *f.* cleaning; cleanliness
limpio,a, clean
listo,a, *a.* ready; clever
llamar, to call
llamarse, to be called
llave, *f.* key
llegar, to arrive
llevar, to take; to carry
llover, to rain
lluvia, *f.* rain
lotería, *f.* lottery
lunes, *m.* Monday
luz, *f.* light

M

madera, *f.* wood
madre, *f.* mother
maduro,a, *a.* mature; ripe
maestro,a, *m., f.* teacher
magnífico,a, *a.* magnificent
malo,a, *a.* bad; sick
maleta, *f.* suitcase
mandar, to send; to order
manejar, to drive; to manage; to handle
mano, *f.* hand
mantener, to maintain
manzana, *f.* apple
mapa, *m.* map
maquillaje, *m.* makeup
maravilloso,a, *a.* marvelous
marcar, to dial; to mark
marcharse, to leave
marisco, *m.* shellfish
martes, *m.* Tuesday
marzo, *m.* March
más, more
matamoscas, *m.* flyswatter
matemática, *f.* mathematics
medianoche, *f.* midnight
mediodía, *m.* noon
medir, to measure
mejor, better
memoria, *f.* memory
menos, less
mentir, to lie
menudo, *m.* tripe; a _____, frequently
mercado, *m.* market
mes, *m.* month
mesa, *f.* table
meter, to put
mexicano,a, *a.* Mexican
miedo, *m.* fear
miércoles, Wednesday
militar, *a.* military
milla, *f.* mile
millón, *m.* million
minuto, *m.* minute

mío,a, *a.* mine
mirar, to look (at)
mi, *a.* my
mismo,a, *a.* same
moda, *f.* fashion
moderno,a, *a.* modern
momento, *m.* moment
morir, to die
motocicleta, *f.* motorcycle
muchacha, *f.* girl
muchacho, *m.* boy
muchedumbre, *f.* crowd
mucho,a, *a.* much; a lot
muebles, *m.* furniture
muerto,a, *a.* dead
mujer, *f.* woman
multitud, *f.* multitude
mundo, *m.* world
museo, *m.* museum
música, *f.* music
muy, *adv.* very

N

nacer, to be born
nación, *f.* nation
nacional, *a.* national
nada, *f.* nothing
nadie, no one
Navidad, *f.* Christmas
necesario,a, *a.* necessary
necesitar, to need
negar, to deny
negarse, to decline, abstain
nervioso,a, *a.* nervous
nevar, to snow
nieve, *f.* snow
ningún,ninguno,a, none; not one; no (*a.*)
niño,a, *m., f.* child
noche, *f.* night
nombre, *m.* name
nosotros, as, we
nota, *f.* grade; note
noticias, *f.* news
novecientos, nine hundred
novela, *f.* novel
novelista, *m., f.* novelist
noveno,a, *a.* ninth
noventa, ninety
novia, *f.* girlfriend; bride
noviembre, November
novio, *m.* boyfriend; groom
nuestro,a, *a.* our
nueve, nine
nuevo,a, new
número, *m.* number
nunca, never

O

obedecer, to obey
obtener, to obtain
ochenta, eighty
ocho, eight

ochocientos, eight hundred
octubre, October
ocupado,a, *a.* busy
ocupar, to occupy; give employment
ofrecer, to offer
oído, *m.* ear (inner)
oír, to hear
ojalá, *interj.* I hope so; God grant that (from Arabic)
ojo, *m.* eye
ola, *f.* wave
oler, to smell
olivar, *m.* olive grove
olvidado,a, *a.* forgotten
olvidar, to forget; olvidarse de + infinitive, to forget to
oportunidad, *f.* opportunity
orden, *f.* order (religious, civil); *m.* order; system
organizar, to organize
origen, *m.* origin
oro, *m.* gold
otoño, *m.* autumn
otro,a, *a.* other

P

pagar, to pay
país, *m.* country (nation)
pájaro, *m.* bird
palabra, *f.* word
palabrota, *f.* swearword
papel, *m.* paper
paquete, *m.* package
para, *prep.* for; _____ + infinitive, in order to
parabrisas, *m.* windshield
paraíso, *m.* paradise
parecer, to seem
pariente,parienta, *m., f.* relative, relation
parque, *m.* park
párrafo, *m.* paragraph
partido, *m.* game; party (political); pact
pasado, *m.* past
pasaje, *m.* passage
pasaporte, *m.* passport
pasar, to pass; to happen; to spend (time)
pasearse, to take a walk
pasión, *f.* passion
patata, *f.* potato
patria, *f.* native land; country
paz, *f.* peace
pedir, to request; to order
peinarse, to comb one's hair
película, *f.* film
pelo, *m.* hair
pelón,na, *a.* bald; *noun (colloq.)* nitwit; penniless
pensar, to think
perder, to lose
perezoso,a, *a.* lazy

perfectamente, *adv.* perfectly
periódico, *m.* newspaper
pero, but
perro,a, *m., f.* dog
perseguir, to pursue, chase; to persecute
persona, *f.* person
peruano,a, *a.* Peruvian
pescado, *m.* fish
pescador, *m.* fisherman
peste, *f.* plague
pintado,a, *a.* painted
pintor, *m.* painter
pintura, *f.* painting
piso, *m.* floor, story (of a building)
planta, *f.* plant
plata, *f.* silver
plátano, *m.* banana
plato, *m.* plate, dish
playa, *f.* beach
pluma, *f.* pen
pobre, *a.* poor
poco,a, *a.* few
poco, *m.* small amount; *adv.* little; not much
poder, to be able
poema, *m.* poem
poeta, *m.* poet
policía, *m.* policeman; *f.* police force
poner, to put
por, *prep.* for; by; through; along
porque, because
portugués,sa, *a.* Portuguese
posible, possible
posesión, *f.* possession
postre, *m.* dessert
práctica, *f.* practice
practicar, to practice
precio, *m.* price
preciso,a, *a.* necessary; precise
preferir, to prefer
pregunta, *f.* question
preguntar, to ask (for information)
preocuparse, to worry
preparar, to prepare
presentación, *f.* presentation
presidente, *m.* president
primavera, *f.* spring
primero,a, *a.* first
prima, *f.* female cousin
primo, *m.* male cousin
principiante, *m., f.* beginner
prisa, *f.* hurry
probar, to prove; to try
problema, *m.* problem
producir, to produce
profesional, *a.* professional
profesor,ra, *m., f.* professor
programa, *m.* program
prometer, to promise
propina, *f.* tip
proyecto, *m.* project
puerta, *f.* door

pues, well; then _____ bien, well then
puesto, *m.* stand; position
pulga, *f.* flea

Q

quedar, to be situated; to stay behind; to be left (over)
quedarse, to remain, to stay; _____ con, to keep, to take
querer, to want
queso, *m.* cheese
quien, who
quienes, who (*pl.*)
química, *f.* chemistry
quinientos, five hundred
quinto,a, *a.* fifth
quitarse, to remove, take off
quizá, quizás, *adv.* maybe, perhaps

R

rápidamente, rapidly
rascacielos, *m.* skyscraper
rata, *f.* rat; *m.* pickpocket
ratón, *m.* mouse
razón, *f.* reason; tener _____, to be right
recibir, to receive
reconocer, to recognize
recordar, to remember; to remind
recuerdo, *m.* memory; souvenir; *pl.* regards
refresco, *m.* refreshment
refrigerador, *m.* refrigerator
regalo, *m.* gift
regresar, to return, go back
reír, to laugh; reírse de, to laugh at; make light of
reloj, *m.* clock, watch
reñir, to quarrel; to scold
repetir, to repeat
representante, *m., f.* representative, agent
resorte, *m.* resort
respetar, to respect
respuesta, *f.* answer
restaurante, *m.* restaurant
resuelto,a, *a.* resolved
resultado, *m.* result
revista, *f.* magazine
rey, *m.* king
rico,a, *a.* rich
roble, *m.* oak
rojo,a, *a.* red
romántico,a, *a.* romantic
romper, to break
roncar, to snore
ropa, *f.* clothing
roto,a, *a.* broken
rubio,a, *a.* blond
ruido, *m.* noise
ruso,a, *a.* Russian

S

sábado, *m.* Saturday
saber, to know; _____ + infinitive, to know how to + verb
sacar, to take out; _____ una foto, to take a photo
sal, *f.* salt; wit; charm; (Cuba) bad luck
sala, *f.* living room; _____ de espera, waiting room
salida, f. exit
salir, to leave; to go out; to come out
saltar, to jump
salud, *f.* health
secretaria, *f.* secretary
secreto, *m.* secret
sed, *f.* thirst
sede, *f.* headquarters
seguida, *f.* succession; en _____, at once
seguir, to continue; to follow
según, according to
segundo,a, *a.* second
seguro,a, *a.* sure; secure, safe
seis, six
seiscientos, six hundred
semana, *f.* week
sentarse, to sit down
sentir, to feel; to regret
septiembre, *m.* September
séptimo,a, *a.* seventh
ser, to be
servir, to serve
sesenta, sixty
setecientos, seven hundred
setenta, seventy
sexto,a, sixth
siempre, always
siete, seven
silla, *f.* chair
sillón, *m.* armchair; easy chair
simpático,a, *a.* nice
sino, but rather; however
sistema, *m.* system
sobre, over; above, on top
soldado, *m.* soldier
soltero, *m.* bachelor
sonámbulo,a, *a.* sleepwalking
sonreir, to smile
sorprender, to surprise
sorteo, *m.* raffle
sostener, to sustain
su, *poss. a.* his, her, your, their
subir, to go up
sucio,a, *a.* dirty
sueco,a, *a.* Swedish
sueldo, *m.* salary
suerte, *f.* luck
sueter, *m.* sweater
suficiente, *a.* sufficient, enough
sufrir, to suffer
sugerir, to suggest
suizo,a, *a.* Swiss

sur, *m.* south
sus, *poss.a.* his; her; your; their
sustituir, to substitute

T

tal, such
también, also
tampoco, neither; either
tanto,a, *a.* so much; *pl.* so many
taquigrafía, *f.* stenography
tarde, *a.* late; *noun f.* afternoon, evening
tarea, *f.* homework
tarjeta, *f.* card
taza, *f.* cup
té, *m.* tea
teatro, *m.* theater
telefonazo, *m.* ring; telephone call
teléfono, *m.* telephone
televisor, *m.* television set
tema, *m.* theme
temblar, to tremble
temprano, early
tener, to have
tenis, *m.* tennis
teoría, *f.* theory
tercer, *a.* third (used before a *m. sing.* noun only)
tercero,a, *a.* third
terminar, to finish
terremoto, *m.* earthquake
testigo, *m.* witness
tía, *f.* aunt
tiburón, *m.* shark
tiempo, *m.* time; weather
tienda, *f.* store
tinto,a, *a.* dyed; *noun m.,* red wine
tío, *m.* uncle
tocadiscos, *m.* record player
tocar, to touch; to play (an instrument, radio, record, etc.)
todavía, *adv.* still; yet; even; _____ no, not yet
todo, *m.* everything
todo,a, *a.* all, every
tomar, to take; to have (food or drink)
tormenta, *f.* storm
toro, *m.* bull
trabajador, *m.* worker
trabajar, to work
trabajo, *m.* work
traducción, *f.* translation
traducir, to translate
traer, to bring
traje, *m.* suit; _____ de baño, bathing suit
trama, *f.* plot
tratar, to treat; _____ de + infinitive, to try to + verb
tratarse (de), to be a question of
trece, thirteen
treinta, thirty

tren, *m.* train
tres, three
trescientos, three hundred
triste, sad
tú, *pron.* (*familiar*) you
tu, *poss. a.* your
tus, *poss a.* your (*plural*)

U

Ud.;Uds, abbreviations for usted, ustedes
últimamente, lately
último,a, *a.* last
una, *a.(f.)* one, a
unas, *a.(f. pl.)* some
único,a, *a.* only; unique
unido,a, *a.* united
universidad, *f.* university
uno, one
unos,as, some
usar, to use; to wear
usted, you (*sing. formal*)
ustedes, you (*pl. formal*)
uva, *f.* grape

V

vacación, *f.* vacation (generally given in *pl.*)
valer, to be worth
vaso, *m.* glass
vecino,a, *m., f.* neighbor
veinte, twenty
veinticinco, twenty-five
veinticuatro, twenty-four
veintidós, twenty-two
veintinueve, twenty-nine
veintiocho, twenty-eight
veintiséis, twenty-six
veintisiete, twenty-seven
veintitrés, twenty-three
veintiuno, twenty-one
velocidad, *f.* speed
vendedor, *m.* salesman
vender, to sell
venezolano,a, *a.* Venezuelan
venir, to come
ventana, *f.* window
ver, to see
verano, *m.* summer
verbo, *m.* verb
verdad, *f.* truth
verde, *a.* green
vestido, *m.* dress
vestir, to dress
vestirse, to get oneself dressed
veterinario,a, *m.,f.* veterinarian
vez, *f.* time, occasion; a veces, at times; una _____, once; dos veces, twice
viajar, to travel
viaje, *m.* trip

vida, *f.* life

viejo,a, *a.* old

viento, *m.* wind

viernes, Friday

vino, *m.* wine

visita, *f.* visit

visitar, to visit

vista, *f.* view

vivir, to live

vivo,a, *a.* alive; lively

volar, to fly

volver, to return

vos, you (*sing. familiar*), substitute for **tú** in some areas of Spanish America

vosotros,as, you (*pl. familiar*), mostly used in Spain

voz, *f.* voice

vuelo, *m.* flight

vuestro,a, *poss. a.* your (*pl. familiar*)

Y

ya, *adv.* already; now; _____ no, no longer; _____ lo creo, I should say so; *interj.* Ya, ya; Oh, yes; I see.

yo, I

Z

zapatería, *f.* shoe store

zapato, *m.* shoe

✓ ABOUT THE AUTHOR

Mary Willix Farmer, M.A., teaches Spanish at the University of California's Extension Program in San Diego. Ms. Farmer began teaching in 1965 as a graduate student at the University of Washington. Since then she has taught at the University of Vermont, Montpelier High School (Montpelier, Vermont), Trinity College, and La Jolla Country Day School (La Jolla, California) and for the San Diego Community College District. Ms. Farmer is a part-time interpreter for California's Department of Social Services and a free-lance translator and writer. She has a B.A. in Spanish from the University of Washington, a certificate in Hispanic Studies from the University of Madrid, and an M.A. in Spanish from the University of Vermont. She has also completed graduate courses at Middlebury College and the University of California, San Diego.